"All the Stories That We Have"

Adolescents' Insights About Literacy and Learning in Secondary Schools

Elizabeth Birr Moje
University of Michigan
Ann Arbor, Michigan, USA

INTERNATIONAL **Reading Association**

800 Barksdale Road, PO Box 8139
Newark, Delaware 19714-8139, USA
www.reading.org

The International Reading Association attempts, through its publications, to provide a forum for a wide spectrum of opinions on reading. This policy permits divergent viewpoints without implying the endorsement of the Association.

Director of Publications   Joan M. Irwin
Assistant Director of Publications   Jeanette K. Moss
Editor in Chief, Books   Matthew W. Baker
Permissions Editor   Janet S. Parrack
Associate Editor   Tori Mello
Publications Coordinator   Beth Doughty
Association Editor   David K. Roberts
Production Department Manager   Iona Sauscermen
Art Director   Boni Nash
Senior Electronic Publishing Specialist   Anette Schütz-Ruff
Electronic Publishing Specialist   Cheryl J. Strum
Electronic Publishing Assistant   Jeanine K. McGann

Project Editor   Tori Mello

Photo Credits   JAM Photography

Library of Congress Cataloging in Publication Data
    Moje, Elizabeth B.
    All the stories that we have: adolescents' insights about literacy and learning in secondary schools/Elizabeth Birr Moje.
        p.   cm.
    Includes bibliographical references and index.
    1. Education, Secondary—Social aspects—United States—Cross-cultural studies.   2. High school students—United States—Social life and customs—Cross-cultural studies.   3. Literacy—Social aspects—United States—Cross-cultural studies.   I. Title.
LC208.4.M65   2000   00-027802
373.18—dc21
ISBN 0-87207-264-9

To John and Avery

Contents

Note From the Series Editor

*I*t is a pleasure to introduce readers to Elizabeth Birr Moje and the eight interesting adolescents she describes in her book. Elizabeth provides powerful stories that shed light on the lives of youth in and out of school, and shows us how these young people use literacy in ways that may go unnoticed or be undervalued by adults who have not had the opportunity to get to know them as individuals and as learners. Elizabeth allows us to hear the voices of these adolescents—honest, proud, yet plaintive voices that are sometimes hard to listen to—that urge us to reconsider how we, as teachers, support learners in and out of our classrooms. I am pleased that Elizabeth's book is one of the first to be published in the Kids InSight series, and I believe it makes a tremendous contribution to the field of adolescent literacy.

The Kids InSight series provides practical information for K–12 teachers and brings to the fore the voices of, and stories about, children and adolescents as the basis for instructional decisions. Books in the series are designed to encourage educators to address the challenge of meeting the literacy needs of all students in our classrooms—as learners and individuals—while recognizing that there are no easy answers or quick fixes to achieving this goal. A sociocultural perspective of how students learn forms the foundation of each Kids InSight book, and authors address learners' emotional, affective, and cognitive development. Dialoguing with other professionals, reading research findings in literacy and education in general, inquiring into teaching and learning processes, observing as well as talking and listening to students, documenting successful practices, and reflecting on literacy events using writing and analysis are strategies and actions embraced by teachers described in the books in this series. Authors of books allow us to see into classrooms and learn about the thoughts and dreams of students as well as the goals and planning processes of teachers. Finally, we are privy to seeing how events actually unfold during formal and informal lessons—the successful and the less-than-successful moments—through the use of transcripts and interview comments woven throughout Kids InSight books.

In *"All the Stories That We Have": Adolescents' Insights About Literacy and Learning in Secondary Schools* Elizabeth shares how she worked to keep kids in sight as she taught adolescents, conducted research in several middle school and high school content classrooms (e.g., science and English, French), and observed and interviewed adolescents outside of school settings. For example, carefully documented stories help us truly see Chile, a young Spanish/Hispanic woman, who moves between the world of her family, the world of student life in a Utah high school, and the world of gang members with whom she "kicks it" or hangs out. At first glance we, as teachers, might dismiss Chile as a problem student—one we are intimidated by because of her attitude, dress, gang affiliations, or because she is from a culture unfamiliar to us. But Elizabeth urges us to look beyond this first glance to see what Chile knows and can do. Chile can tell wonderful oral stories but is not as anxious to craft them into written texts at school. In interviews with Chile, Elizabeth gleans insights about members of Chile's family, all of whom love stories, both oral and written. In fact, Chile's mother wanted to write stories and urged Chile to write a book with her because, as her mom emphasized, it is important to document "all the stories we have" as a family. By looking closely and reconsidering new ideas about literacy learning and teaching, we see that Chile draws on family and cultural knowledge bases as she engages in school tasks. Throughout her book, Elizabeth challenges us to consider how we might build on this cultural knowledge as we work with learners.

While reading Elizabeth's book I found myself questioning a lot of my beliefs about adolescents and rethinking my practices. I was dismayed when I read adolescents' reports of feeling silenced and dismissed in their classes at school, and I wondered how many times I inadvertently contributed to these same feelings in adolescents I have interacted with. I believe strongly in the need to build caring relationships with students, as outlined by Elizabeth, and the need to offer them challenging and meaningful learning experiences in which they learn to question societal structures and practices that privilege some individuals and disenfranchise others. Elizabeth effectively transports readers to another world—the world of adolescents—and helps us understand the thinking, emotions, and lives of these young people. As Elizabeth notes, our role as teachers is to help students see that "what they do in and out of school matters...that they matter and that they can make a difference in the world."

Deborah R. Dillon
Series Editor
Purdue University
West Lafayette, Indiana, USA

Kids InSight Review Board

Melvin L. Thursby
Prairie Middle School
Cedar Rapids, Iowa, USA

Jan Turbill
University of Wollongong
Wollongong, New South Wales,
    Australia

Angela Ward
University of Saskatchewan
Saskatoon, Saskatchewan,
    Canada

Deborah A. Wooten
Glenwood Landing School
Glen Head, New York, USA

Josephine P. Young
Arizona State University
Tempe, Arizona, USA

Acknowledgments

Many young people, teaching and research colleagues, friends, and family members have been an integral part of the writing of this book. For sharing their lives with me—in and out of school—I thank the youth and the three exemplary teachers represented in this book. I am also grateful to the three anonymous reviewers who provided detailed critical feedback for improving the manuscript.

Similarly, the Kids InSight Series Editor, Deborah R. Dillon, and the authors of *Looking Through the Faraway End: Creating a Literature-Based Reading Curriculum With Second Graders*—Lee Galda, Lisa Cross Stanzi, and Shane Rayburn—provided critical feedback and generative conversation throughout the writing process.

The staff at the International Reading Association—Tori Mello, Matt Baker, and Joan Irwin—were also incredibly generous and inspirational with their support, guidance, and patience in this process. Special thanks to Tori, who perservered through my stubborn refusals to change even the smallest of words.

In addition, I thank the many literacy scholars and educators with whom I've been associated in the last 17 years. Although we may not have interacted on this book explicitly, their teaching and research have shaped what I have been able to say about literacy. Many of them are cited throughout the text. I could often feel each of these individuals reading over my shoulder and nudging me to select just the right words, to tell just the right stories that would make a difference in the lives of adolescents. If I've succeeded in that endeavor, all of these people deserve the credit as much as I do.

Finally, I thank John Moje and Avery Birr Moje, who inspired me, supported me, and really *did* read over my shoulder throughout the writing of this book.

Chapter 1

Learning From Kids

Since I have been in this writing class, I have been reintroduced to the joys of reading books. I have read over fifteen books and countless short stories in the past year. This is great because I haven't read a book since I got out of high school.   *Charles, age 31*

This quote, from a former student at an adult literacy academy, was a catalyst in my decision to be a different kind of teacher. When Charles spoke these words to me, I had been teaching adults for about 2 years. Prior to that teaching experience, I had taught high school history and biology in traditional high school settings, and literacy to young people in alternative high school settings. Charles's stories, together with the stories of a number of students at the adult literacy academy, taught me a great deal that I had not known about teaching before that time. As one young woman I worked with stated in an interview, "I think it would be so nice [to write a book] because of all the stories that we have." Her words, along with the stories and comments of many other adolescents and young adults, inspired the title of this book, which focuses on adolescents' stories and their insights about teaching and learning in—and often out of—secondary schools.

One of the most poignant stories came from Rick, a struggling reader and writer who, upon receiving a merit certificate for completion of an academy basic literacy class, said to me, "I've never been to anything like this. I've never gotten an award for school." And yet, Rick had a successful life as a builder outside of school, success that gave him the strength and self-respect to live a meaningful and happy life, despite the struggles he had experienced in school. (See Box 1-1 for further accounts of the experiences of adult literacy learners.) It frustrated me to see that his experiences and strengths outside of school had been discounted and devalued. These teaching experiences reinforced my conviction that good teaching—especially when teaching people who are often marginalized in school and society—should draw from and expand on the experiences, texts, values, and ideas that adolescents bring to school, thereby allowing students to experience school success in a variety of ways. Although I had experience in high school settings prior to my adult literacy teaching, it was my experience with adults who had struggled or not been engaged in high school that inspired my passion and commitment to excellence in secondary school teaching and encouraged me to conduct research on how to provide successful and rich learning experiences for adolescent students. This book draws from that research and is based on the premise that young people have important stories to tell—stories that we can learn from, be responsive to, and bring into our classrooms to serve as texts for teaching and learning.

Reflection Point

In the next section I present my goals for writing this book. Before going on, however, I encourage you to obtain a journal and write in it the most memorable stories from, or interactions with, a student in your own teaching career. Then take a minute to reflect on and analyze what these words or experiences have meant to you in your teaching. Why did you choose this particular student? Why these words or this event? What do these words, actions, or interactions say about you as a teacher?

Keep this personal anecdote in mind as you read this book, and compare your own students' stories with those of the students I represented in this text. Consider how the stories are similar or differ.

> **BOX 1-1**
> **Further Reading About Adult Literacy Learners**
> There are a number of interesting accounts told from the perspective of people who had not been successful in school. I have found such accounts useful in rethinking my teaching because they have given me insights into what young people were experiencing. For example Peter Johnston's (1985) presentation of three stories of adult literacy learners reveals the specific difficulties that these adults had experienced as young people learning to read. Other accounts of adult learners include Guerra, 1997; Kazemek, 1988; and Oates, 1998.

Why Am I Writing This Book?

> Classes might have been a little better if most of my teachers would
> have made learning a little more interesting.
> Charles, 1990

As a way of grounding this discussion of teaching and learning in kids' insights, needs, and interests, in this book I share the stories of students I have taught and of young people who have worked with me in research projects. Although I foreground kids' insights from these stories, I also draw from reflections on my own teaching, from the extensive knowledge base of teachers with whom I've worked as a researcher, and from the research of others to make four primary suggestions for reframing secondary literacy teaching. Because my commitment to responsive teaching grows out of learning about youth over the last 15 years—learning about their lives, their passions, and the literacies that matter to them—I present their words and experiences in as unadulterated a form as possible. My primary goal in presenting adolescents' lives and experiences is to show the importance of understanding their literacy practices and experiences and to generate ideas for how we can bring young people's practices to bear on teaching and curriculum development so that we are responsive teachers. A second goal is to advance the idea that all children need strong, abiding relationships with adults, and as teachers and researchers we are in a position to build such relationships. Consequently, I suggest that part of secondary teaching—whether of literacy processes and practices or of content concepts—needs to focus on the development of caring relationships that make spaces for young people to inquire, speak, read, write, and perform what they are interested in and care about. At the same time, however, caring should not take the form of letting students do whatever they want; caring relationships also push students to examine new ideas, learn new skills, and build new relationships.

I also hope to illustrate that being literate involves more than just being able to read and write print, and to show how literacy practices are laden with social, cultural, and institutional values. To accomplish this goal, I will highlight the importance of understanding how race, class, gender, and cultural relations shape teaching and learning. Young people in classrooms today talk openly about race, class, gender, and culture. They also talk and act at times in oppressive and discriminatory ways. It is important that as teachers we are able to talk and work with youth to address issues of race, class, gender, and culture in ways that will support their growth as fair-minded, ethical, and empowered human beings. One way to work toward this goal is to weave the teaching and learning of literacy and content into critical, inquiry-based projects in which young people examine issues or questions of interest to them so that they can begin to see a larger purpose for education. If possible, these projects should be developed to cross or integrate the different disciplines, so that what students learn in one class is linked to what they learn in another class. Moreover, these projects should extend beyond the school walls so that students see themselves as active members of a community, members whose actions and beliefs count for something. Finally, as we engage adolescents in critical project-based pedagogy that is based on what they know and care about, we should draw from the texts they value and offer them many different texts and tools to represent their understanding and to help them gain access to many different communities and opportunities.

A fourth goal of this book is to make evident what good teachers already know: There are no easy, simple answers in teaching. Instead, what is referred to as "best practice" in teaching requires listening to and learning from young people, learning and experimenting with many different teaching strategies, and making difficult decisions—often on the spot—about how to help youth learn to use a variety of literacy skills that will allow them to become successful and contributing members of an equitable society. It is my hope that making this point in a public forum will support teachers as they meet social and political challenges to their autonomy as decision makers who have the best interests of adolescents at heart.

Finally, I hope to bring theory and research to practice in a useful, readable, and engaging manner. Throughout my career I have grown as a teacher by reading theories and research that relate to teaching. I have also grown by learning to articulate my own theories and by doing research on my own and others' practice. But, as the saying goes, theory without practice is dead. It does not go anywhere or accomplish anything in the real, material lives of teachers and students. In this book, I subscribe to Paulo Freire's (1970) idea of *praxis*. That is, like Freire, I believe that reflection and action must work together in a relationship wherein reflection informs and shapes action, but action also informs and shapes reflection. In praxis, one engages in a kind of reflective action that is not merely reflection (theory) nor action (practice), but a unique and generative combination of the two. To encourage the development of praxis as a result of reading this book, I make evident the changes in my own thinking and practice over time. I hope that readers will also engage in different kinds of practice and reflect—systematically and informally— on these practices.

Who Are the People Represented in This Book?

> I hate science, but I love Ms. Landy.
>
> Noreen, 1993

> I mean, I enjoy science and I'll read what's assigned just cause I like it. It's not boring to me. It's kind of interesting.
>
> Lew, 1992

> School's boring.
>
> Anthony, 1997

> I love school.
>
> Staci, 1993

> This is why I hate school so much, all I get is Ds and Fs.
>
> Tricia, 1995

> I would do whatever anybody told me to do....'Cause I just wanted, I've always, 'cause they were popular people in our school, and I wanted to be popular, you know?
>
> Katie, 1997

> I don't fit in with high school people.
>
> Heather, 1992

The comments from young people that begin this section represent the range of different kinds of youth portrayed throughout this book (all names are pseudonyms). They come from different ethnic, cultural, and religious backgrounds. They are different colors and come from different socioeconomic backgrounds as well. Both young men and young women are represented. They range in age from 12 to 18 years (adolescence, technically defined, covers the ages 10 to 20 years). Some care deeply about school and see it as an important path to success later in life; others are biding their time, or even openly resisting the accepted practices of the school by getting involved in gangs or other unsanctioned practices. Some are actually interested in the content being taught, while others participate because they like their teachers. Some want to be "popular" and others wish they didn't have to put up with their peers. I use this range to illustrate that despite our emphasis on general patterns in education (you'll find me emphasizing some patterns in this book), young people are unique individuals with needs that differ in important ways. At the same time, each adolescent is situated in and shaped by particular social, cultural, and political relationships. Some come to school privileged simply by their color or their social class; others fight stereotypes about who they are on a daily basis. So even as teachers need to consider adolescents as individuals, we must also consider that individuals are socially constructed beings.

For example, Tricia, whose voice is represented in the quotes that open this section, is a waif-like Latina from a working-class home. Tricia has struggled in school all her life. Each time she receives a D or an F, she also receives a message that she is not cut out for school. Staci, also quoted in the opening, is, by contrast, a tall, muscular European American girl whose parents are educators. Her school experiences have always been positive. She knows how to participate in class discussions, and knows what to say and how to say it to draw teachers' attention and interest. It is little wonder that she "loves school." How much of the difference between these two girls is a result of their individual cognitive ability, and how much is a consequence of their differing life practices? How much is a consequence of institutional structures and practices that support certain ways of being, acting, reading, and writing, and dismiss other ways? These are some of the questions that this book will tackle as it examines what adolescents have to say about their literacy practices and their school experiences.

This general description provides a sense of who the kids were as a group, but there are a few young people on whom I rely heavily to offer insights for secondary school literacy teaching; I would like to describe each of them in more depth. In addition, three teachers were generous enough to let me do research in their classrooms, and they deserve description in this chapter. Finally, I will tell you something explicit about myself so that you will have a clear sense of my background and biases as you read the remainder of this book. I begin by introducing the key players: the eight adolescents who shared their lives with me in various ways.

The Adolescents

These eight young people come from different places and had very different relationships with me. One young woman is someone I taught, someone who in turn taught me a great deal about teaching and about the importance of reaching out to have a presence in the lives of young people. The others are all from classroom research studies. Four of the youths also worked with me for 2 years outside the classroom in which I met them, and so have shaped my teaching and research in immeasurable ways (see Moje, 1999). I will describe each of these students by writing about what stood out in my relationships with them. As much as I have tried to make the descriptions parallel in nature, I cannot, because my relationship with each student was different. Further, because I want to emphasize the importance of acting in relation with adolescents, rather than lumping them into categories and patterns, I have chosen to retain the difference in these descriptions.

Jane. Jane was my student during my second and third years of teaching high school. I taught her in two different classes, and I directed her in a school play. Jane is a White, European American woman from a middle-class background. As a high school student she was gifted as a performer and artist, but she was also troubled and lonely. She was not marginalized to the same extent that some teens are (for example, the young men of the 1999 Columbine High School tragedy in Denver, Colorado), but she fought a sense of estrangement and of uncertainty about her life and her goals. A well-adjusted and good student on the outside, she struggled on the inside, a struggle that she did not fully reveal to me until many years later when she wrote me a series of letters to tell me how much my support—which I did not realize I had given—had meant to her during her adolescent years.

Mike. Mike was a student in a fourth-year high school French class that I studied for one semester in 1990 (see Moje, Brozo, & Haas, 1994). A tall, lanky, White European American male, Mike came from an upper–middle-class home in a U.S. midwestern state. As a student in the class, Mike participated in a portfolio project experiment (and research study) that the teacher, Jayne Haas, conducted with Bill Brozo and me. Our idea was to use portfolios as both learning and assessment tools. Students were asked to identify a topic related to the French language or culture and to study it by reading, writing, interviewing people, watching videos, and listening to music. All discourse—both oral and written—connected with the project was to be conducted in French. The project led to a small rebellion in the class, with Mike as one of the most vocal dissenters. Mike's displeasure with the project centered around the amount of time it would take him to engage in the research. He made it clear that he had enrolled in this fourth year of French to provide a break in his difficult, honors-student schedule. Like many of his classmates, he wanted to do the "book work" to which he had become accustomed in previous years of French class, because he found it more manageable than the thinking and communicating necessary for the innovative portfolio projects.

Heather. I met Heather during one year of my 2^1/$_2$-year qualitative study of literacy practices in a chemistry classroom (see Moje, 1996). A diminutive, White, 16-year-old female, Heather came from a middle-class home in a U.S. midwestern state. Like Mike, her ethnic background was European American. I noticed her in the class right away because, unlike most of the other students, Heather engaged in conversation with another female student in the class, or she wrote notes to people outside of class. Other than the student with whom Heather chatted, students in the chemistry class rarely talked during the class activities, except to answer questions posed by the teacher or to ask questions. Also interesting about Heather is that when the teacher called on her, Heather was always able to answer questions appropriately. I learned that although she seemed distracted in class, Heather always did the reading, used the reading/note-taking strategy that the teacher had taught early in the year, and asked herself deep questions about the nature of the physical world (although she did not ask these questions in class). These habits made Heather an interesting student, especially in contrast to Mike, who only engaged in activities to get a grade.

Chile. Chile was a student in the Salt Lake City (Utah) junior high school English classroom that I studied in 1995 (see Moje, Willes, & Fassio, in press), and she became a member of a 2-year research project that I conducted on adolescents' literacy practices out of school (see Moje, in press). Over the 3 years we worked together, I watched her grow from a sharp, assertive child into a tremulous young woman concerned with her body and sexuality. Chile identified as Spanish/Hispanic but acknowledged some Mexican heritage. Her mother and grandmother both grew up in New Mexico. Her family members see themselves as American—at times looking with disdain on recent immigrants from Mexico—but they maintain Hispanic cultural practices and attend a Spanish Catholic church. Chile claimed that she could not speak Spanish, but she was able to talk with her grandmother in Spanish, and she easily interpreted the Spanish spoken at Mass when I went with her. When I first met Chile, she appeared to be a model, mainstream student, although teachers commented on her gang-connected dress styles. Throughout her seventh- and eighth-grade years, however, Chile became more and more identified with gangs. In ninth grade, Chile transferred to a different school, adopted a different style of dress, and resisted outward gang identification. She continued, however, to "kick it," or hang out socially with gang members. Chile and I became very close throughout our research together, and we maintain a friendship today.

Khek. Khek was also a student from Salt Lake City and a participant in both my in-school and out-of-school research projects. A thin, brown-skinned young woman, Khek identified herself as "Laos" (rather than as Laotian). Her parents and an older brother and sister had left Laos for Thailand before Khek was born. They then emigrated from Thailand to the United States when Khek was 5 years old. Although Khek and her siblings speak fluent English, Khek's parents speak little English. At the time of my study, the family lived in a two-bedroom apartment in an area of Salt Lake City commonly referred to as "Little Saigon." Like Chile, when our relationship began Khek was involved in gang practices—particularly gang writing (e.g., graffiti) and gang dress (such as baggy pants, windbreaker, a certain type of sports shoe identified as "gangsta Nikes" by the youth). As she grew older, she rejected gang practices and membership, but maintained affiliations with gang members. In class, Khek appeared disengaged from the reading and writing activities of the literacy workshop approach, despite the fact that these activities were designed to engage the students in writing about their own experiences. Outside of class Khek was most interested in boys and expensive cars. When I asked her what she would like to do in her English class, she said that she enjoyed worksheets that asked her questions about the stories she had read.

Jeffrey. Jeffrey, a third student in the English classroom and out-of-school literacy studies in Salt Lake City, identified himself as part Mexican, part Hispanic. Like Chile, he traced his ancestry to Spain, but he privileged his Mexican roots, telling stories learned from his grandfather of how the "White man" massacred the Indians who lived in Mexico. Although small in stature and seemingly immature in school interactions (for instance, he often yelled out as teachers spoke), Jeffrey frequently made insightful comments during class discussions about the novels we were reading. Jeffrey, however, was identified as a problem student because he was so active during class and because he was often late for school or was truant. In his eighth-grade year, Jeffrey was moved to an alternative school program housed within the junior high school building. Jeffrey found that program much more to his liking, stating that the teacher was difficult but seemed to be willing to let students do things they were interested in.

Mark. Mark, a student from Salt Lake City, identified himself as "biracial" because his mother is Hawaiian and his father is African American. Although Mark had some gang connections, he also was a participant in a Saturday school program offered by a local Baptist church. As part of the Saturday school program, he not only attended classes but also participated in an African drumming troupe. In his public school classes, Mark encountered a number of difficulties due to his struggle to attend to class discussions or activities and because of his failure to complete assignments. Like Jeffrey, Mark often made insightful comments, but he usually interrupted others to do so or he couched comments in loud, joking tones in what seemed like an effort to be viewed as the class clown. Mark participated only in the second semester of the English classroom research study, and although he was interested in participating in the out-of-school study, we were never able to arrange times that we could spend together.

Anthony. Anthony was 12 years old and described his ethnicity as "Viet." He dressed routinely in baggy pants, a blue windbreaker, and white sneakers (what other students called "gangsta Nikes"). He lived with his mother and two younger brothers in a neighborhood near the school in which I conducted the English classroom literacy study. His family spoke a mixture of English and Vietnamese, but Anthony spoke fluent English. When Anthony first arrived in the seventh-grade English class, he seemed reticent and shy, but not uncooperative. He attended class regularly, engaged in various activities, and produced a number of written products. When reading class novels, he appeared to follow along, ready to read if chosen by another student. He read clearly and fluently, but without expression or excitement. In his early class writings, Anthony described school as long and boring. In later writings, Anthony described gang-connected activities in great detail, although he never implicated himself as a full participant in the practices. His end-of-the-year social action project in the class focused on graffiti and gang violence, and in our research together over the next year, Anthony demonstrated a great deal of knowledge of gang practices.

These young people, along with others whose voices or experiences fill this book, have made an important impact on my teaching, as well as on my thinking about adolescence, literacy, and secondary schooling. Their insights form the basis of this book. I expect that most readers—whether novice teachers or veterans—can recall young people who stand out in their experience. This book is about trying to reflect systematically on those experiences to serve as guideposts for responsive and planful literacy pedagogy.

*Reflection Point*_____

Write a description of the student you reflected on at the beginning of this chapter. Now reread your description. What did you
focus on? What made this student memorable for you? What did
you learn about teaching from this student? How did he or she
shape your beliefs about teaching, learning, literacy, or your content area? What do you know about that student as a person outside your classroom?

_____

The Teachers

Three other people are also critically important in this book. They are
the teachers with whom I've conducted research: Jayne Haas, a high
school French teacher; Dorothy Landy, a high school chemistry teacher;
and Diane Wilson, a junior high school English teacher (like the student
names, Landy and Wilson are both pseudonyms; the nature of research
with Haas was different from the other two projects, and we have retained
her given name in our other publications).

Because my relationship with each teacher was very different—I was
more of an observer-participant in Landy's classroom and more of a
participant-observer in Jayne's and Diane's classrooms—I will refer to
the three teachers in different ways throughout the text, calling Jayne
and Diane by first names, but referring to Landy by her last name. A
colleague, Bill Brozo, and I worked with Jayne for one semester to develop a portfolio project approach to teaching and learning French. As explained in the previous description of the young man Mike, a number of
things went wrong as we tried this innovative practice, and we all learned
a great deal from our struggle that semester. I worked with Landy for $2^1/_2$
years while I conducted dissertation research; my focus in her classroom
was on how she used various content area literacy strategies to help students learn chemistry. Diane and I worked together to develop, enact, and
study a literacy workshop and project-based pedagogy in her seventh-
grade English classroom. All three of these educators taught me a great

deal about teaching by allowing me to study their classrooms and their pedagogy. I write this book as a tribute to them, as well as to the young people with whom they worked.

The Author: Teacher and Researcher

I am a former high school teacher turned university teacher educator and researcher. I started my teaching career as a high school biology, history, and government teacher (I even taught typing for 2 years), and I later taught alternative high school and adult literacy courses. I became interested in content area or secondary literacy teaching and learning when I found that my high school students either would not read or could not read well. As I studied for a master's degree in literacy, I found myself wondering why more high school teachers were not concerned with this issue. I also found myself wondering about how excellent secondary school teachers put the ideas they learned in literacy courses into practice in their actual classrooms. Most secondary literacy research has focused on testing whether teaching strategies developed by literacy researchers are effective in classrooms, but these strategies have been tested under controlled conditions. My work, on the other hand, has examined what teachers and students actually do to make sense of and enact strategies. Guided by a number of scholars and mentors in the field, I brought a social and cultural lens to secondary and adolescent literacy research. (For a listing of scholars who've conducted groundbreaking work in this area, see Box 1-2 on page 14.)

My questions about what really happens in classrooms led me to conduct qualitative research in high school and, eventually, junior high school classrooms. All my studies have focused on how teachers' and students' beliefs about and practices of literacy shape their interpretations and enactments of various literacy pedagogies (such as project-based pedagogy, writer's workshop, and strategies instruction). I have conducted three such studies in secondary classrooms and have participated in two other studies conducted in upper-level (fourth and fifth grade) elementary classrooms. In each case, I have focused on how teachers and students interact when they engage in innovative pedagogy, and on what they bring to those interactions. The methods I use in each study include participant observation, interviewing, and the collection of documents and ar-

BOX 1-2
Further Reading About the Sociocultural Contexts of Literacy

If you are interested in reading other studies that have explored the social and cultural contexts of secondary literacy teaching and learning, you might wish to consult some of these texts:

Bloome, D. (1989). *Classrooms and literacy*. Norwood, NJ: Ablex.

Dillon, D.R. (1989). Showing them that I want them to learn and that I care about who they are: A microethnography of social organization of a secondary low-track English-reading classroom. *American Educational Research Journal, 26*, 227–259.

Dillon, D.R., O'Brien, D.G., Moje, E.B., & Stewart, R.A. (1994). Literacy learning in secondary school science classrooms: A cross-case analysis of three qualitative studies. *Journal of Research in Science Teaching, 31*, 345–362.

Dillon, D.R., & Moje, E.B. (1998). Listening to the talk of adolescent girls: Lesson about literacy, school, and lives. In D.E. Alvermann, K.A. Hinchman, D.W. Moore, S.F. Phelps, & D.R. Waff (Eds.), *Reconceptualizing the literacies in adolescents' lives* (pp. 193–224). Mahwah, NJ: Erlbaum.

Egan-Robertson, A. (1998). Learning about culture, language, and power. *Journal of Literacy Research, 30*(4), 449–487.

Gee, J.P. (1990). *Social linguistics and literacies: Ideology in discourses*. London: Falmer Press.

Heath, S.B. (1983). *Ways with words: Language, life, and work in communities and classrooms*. Cambridge, UK: Cambridge University Press.

Hinchman, K.A., & Zalewski, P. (1996). Reading for success in a tenth grade global studies class: A qualitative study. *Journal of Literacy Research, 28*(1), 91–106.

Knobel, M. (1999). *Everyday literacies*. New York: Lang.

Lankshear, C., with Gee, J.P., Knobel, M., & Searle, C. (1997). *Changing literacies*. Buckingham, UK: Open University Press.

Myers, J. (1992). The social contexts of school and personal literacy. *Reading Research Quarterly, 27*, 296–333.

O'Brien, D.G. (1998). Multiple literacies in a high school program for "at-risk" adolescents. In D.E. Alvermann, K.A. Hinchman, D.W. Moore, S.F. Phelps, & D.R. Waff (Eds.), *Reconceptualizing the literacies in adolescents' lives* (pp. 27–49). Mahwah, NJ: Erlbaum.

Santa Barbara Discourse Group. (1994). Constructing literacy in classrooms: Literate action as social accomplishment. In R.B. Ruddell, M.R. Ruddell, & H. Singer (Eds.), *Theoretical models and processes of reading* (4th ed., pp. 124–154). Newark, DE: International Reading Association.

tifacts I use a variety of qualitative analysis techniques, but these most often include constant comparative analysis, as described by Glaser and Strauss (1967) and discourse analysis (Cazden, 1988; Fairclough, 1992, Gee, Michaels, & O'Connor, 1992; Luke, 1995/1996).

My most recently completed study extended beyond the classroom into the lives of several young people. Late in 1994, as I began my fifth major classroom-based research study, a colleague challenged me with two questions that dramatically reshaped my teaching and research. "Why," he demanded, "do you study literacy in schools and classrooms? Do you assume that all literacy learning happens there?" His questions haunted me, and I could not dismiss them as I continued to plan my research project. I had drawn from research conducted outside of classrooms, research that shows disjunctures between the uses of literacy valued in school and the ways people read, write, and talk in homes and communities. In my own teaching and in my classroom-based research, I had valued the out-of-school lives of my own students. Why, then, did I not make outside-of-school research an explicit component of my work?

My colleague's questions prompted me to think back over my teaching and research career. I began teaching high school biology and history in 1983, with the extracurricular assignment of directing the school's dramatic productions. The chance to work with adolescents in non-classroom settings, in which they drew on intelligences and knowledges not usually privileged in the classroom, afforded me an opportunity to learn about students' strengths and helped me connect curricula to students' lives. These experiences—in two middle-class, diverse, private schools—taught me to value what adolescents could do outside of school and to stretch as a teacher by building curricula designed to tap into and expand students' strengths and interests. When I changed jobs to work with students who often lived in poverty and had not succeeded in traditional school settings, I was forced to rethink what teaching meant. I learned how young people had been shut out of academic, social, and community opportunities because they could not successfully perform the academic tasks deemed valuable in school. I learned that in many cases these young people had been shut out not on the basis of their performance, but on the basis of physical or social markers such as ethnicity, class, or gender.

Even with these experiences, my early research focused primarily on how and why literacy was used in secondary school classrooms, specifically in French, social studies, and chemistry classrooms. But in my most recent research, a year-long study of two English classrooms in an urban junior high school, the students themselves pushed me out of the school and into their lives. As I began to collect classroom data, I noted that students at times kept their academic and social literacy practices separate, "code switching" between what they seemed to believe were acceptable topics and writing styles during the writer's workshop and what they believed were acceptable topics and writing styles in casual notes to friends or on notebooks, walls, desks, and bodies.

I was particularly interested in the students who were identified and identified themselves as "gangstas" or as affiliated with gangs. As I watched these gang-connected youth use literacy, I was intrigued with the contradiction I saw between their motivation to rapidly internalize very specific and complicated gang writing styles, spellings, rules, and dress codes, and their seeming indifference to using conventional writing style, spelling, punctuation, and grammar. I began to wonder what these uses of literacy meant for adolescents, both in terms of their social and cultural lives and in terms of their learning of standard literacy practices. It was through this interest in how their unsanctioned, social literacies merged with their academic literacies that I finally acted on my belief that what happens in kids' lives out of school is as important as what happened in schools and classrooms. Consequently, I conducted a 2-year study of the literacy lives of six youths outside of school, with a focus on how they used unsanctioned literacies to make meaning. All were members of the English classroom in which I had conducted a year of research focused on literacy workshop practices, and all are described on the previous pages and represented in the remainder of the book.

Thus, this book has grown out of a long-term research agenda, combined with my own secondary school and adult literacy teaching experiences and with my university teaching. Too often we forget that teacher education involves teaching, and that we must draw from preservice and inservice teachers' insights as we plan teacher education. One of my goals as a teacher educator has been to always keep in sight the fact that I remain a teacher regardless of what educational level I teach. This book has helped me keep that goal alive. In this light, I have endeavored to write this book about kids' insights based on the insights, concerns, and questions that I have heard from the teachers I work with in university courses. And I hope that it contributes to the education of all teachers who read it.

In the next chapter I will discuss some of my central beliefs about literacy, adolescents, and the secondary school. I invite you to reflect on your own beliefs, compare them to mine, and construct for yourself a well-articulated belief statement that you will continue to revisit as you read the insights of young people and the ideas for practice offered throughout the book.

Chapter 2

Adolescent Literacies in the Secondary School: Beliefs and Practices

> *Elizabeth sits in the third row, fourth seat, of the English classroom, madly scribbling field notes during a discussion of a novel. As she looks up to glance at the classroom clock so that she can time date her notes, she happens to see both Anthony (a student) and Diane (the teacher) also casting surreptitious glances at the clock. She is struck by the irony that both teacher and student are watching the clock during a class discussion. What are they thinking as they check the time? "Am I going to get them through this chapter in time?" "How much longer do we have to sit here?" "What do I have planned for next period?" "What class do I have to go to next period?"*
>
> *And what is Elizabeth, as researcher in the classroom, thinking as she glances at the clock? Why is it important to note the time that events occur in a classroom? What is it about secondary classrooms that makes them so time oriented? Why are we all watching the clock? How does the clock control each of us in different ways? What would we rather be doing?*

What I Believe About Secondary School Literacy Teaching and Learning

This vignette represents for me some of the exigencies of secondary school teaching: a focus, for example, on time, control, and content coverage. I can easily imagine the teacher, Diane, looking at the clock to see how much time she had left for this discussion before she needed to turn to another activity that she hoped to complete. I can see her calculating the number of pages left in the chapter by the number of minutes left in the period. I can imagine her thinking ahead to her next period, perhaps a different subject area, and running through her mind what she will be teaching in that class.

On the other hand, this vignette also represents a common student perspective. I can envision Anthony thinking about how much longer he had to sit there as the discussion swirled about him, how much time he had left before he could leave the class to go talk to people in the hall, before sitting through his next class, or before leaving the building to hang out with his friends at the park or galleria. Alternatively, I can imagine him glancing at the clock to see how much time was left before math class, in which he would have to take a test for which he had not studied!

Although many people, whether students or teachers, have probably found themselves watching the clock in a classroom, we rarely stop to ask ourselves why the secondary school is set up in this way, or to ask what we really believe about how and in what settings adolescents might learn best. As teachers, we also rarely take time to think about what adolescents might be doing or thinking about when they are not in our classrooms. Throughout my years of teaching and my study of teaching and learning, I have come to believe that teaching and research need to be based on a carefully articulated, but always developing, philosophy of education. This philosophy is based on what I believe about *knowledge* in my content areas of expertise, about *learning*, about *adolescents*, and about *literacy*.

For example, I view knowledge in my content areas of expertise (history, political science, biology, and literacy) as sets of ideas that are constructed over time by people as they engage in various activities and practices. Knowledge is more than information or facts because it is always connected to the practices and activities in which people engage. Learning, then, is the act of engaging in those practices and participating in acts of knowledge construction and reconstruction. Adolescents are people who are learning to become full participants in those practices and, as such, they are constructing and reconstructing the ideas that are already established. Given these other perspectives, literacy can be seen both as one of those practices that serves to construct and reconstruct

knowledge, and also as sets of tools that can be used within other practices. (I expand on this definition of literacy in a later section.)

Teacher-education students often express dismay when I ask them to
articulate their philosophical perspectives in these areas, but as they begin
to talk and write about their thinking, they come to see that teaching is always shaped by beliefs and philosophies. Research has illustrated—and I
have learned on a personal level—that if teachers are not consciously
aware of the subtleties of the beliefs and experiences that guide their practice, then they will be less likely to change in response to students' needs
and interests. Consequently, I find it very important to think about, write
about, and present my own beliefs as a teacher and teacher educator.

*Reflection Point*_____

**Before you read my perspectives, take some time to write and re-
flect on your beliefs about knowledge in your content area, learning, adolescents, and literacy. (It might be useful to try to come
up with a metaphor to represent each of these areas.) Then "observe yourself" for a day and jot down all the different ways you
use literacy (you might want to make a video for easier observation). In what ways are these uses of literacy tied to your beliefs
about knowledge, adolescents, and learning?**

_____

My beliefs about teaching and learning literacy revolve around four
major points: (1) an acknowledgment of how literacy is used differently in
secondary school than it is in elementary school, (2) an understanding of
how adolescents use literacy in and out of school, (3) a broad understanding of literacy as involving more than the reading and writing of
written text, and (4) a belief that literacy teaching in secondary schools
needs to be responsive to adolescents' unique needs and driven by the organization of concepts and ideas.

Before turning to a discussion of these points, however, a brief discussion of the term *literacy*, and a related phrase, *literacy practices*, is in

order. The word *literacy* has a contested history, and definitions of the term are numerous, both in scholarly and popular literatures. One useful perspective is Venezky's (1995) definition from *The Literacy Dictionary*:

> Literacy is a minimal ability to read and write in a designated language, as well as a mindset or way of thinking about the use of reading and writing in everyday life. It differs from simple reading and writing in its assumption of an understanding of the appropriate use of these abilities within a print-based society. (p. 142)

What makes Venezky's definition useful is his refusal to conclude the definition of literacy with the ability to read and write in a designated language. His inclusion of ways of thinking about the uses of reading and writing links his definition in important ways to the definitions offered by those who refer to literacy *practices*—or the values, beliefs, and actions that people bring to reading and writing (see Barton, 1994; Gee, 1996; Scribner & Cole, 1981; Street, 1984).

Where Venezky's definition falls short, however, is in his association of literacy only with print, and in his failure to emphasize the social and political nature of literacy and literacy practices. Although I prefer to use the term *literacy* to refer to the reading and writing of written text, I also believe that we must broaden the sense of what it means to be literate and to use reading and writing. In particular, I think that we can view text quite broadly, so that a musical score or a choreographed dance can be considered a written text. In addition, literacy is a social act; even when individuals read alone they read with social purposes, in social contexts, and with social meanings attached to the reading that they do.

People are positioned in certain ways—allowed to construct certain identities—in accordance with both how literate they are considered to be and with the types or ways of literacy they practice. Street (1994) uses the example of the reading and writing done by housewives; he argues that such reading is not accorded the same prestige and value as the reading and writing done by doctors. Similarly, the reading and writing done in an upper-level history course may be seen as more sophisticated and important than the reading and writing done in a physical education course. Or the novels that adolescents choose to read in their free time may be considered less valuable than the classic novels offered in their literature courses. These positionings allow or restrict access to social situations and material goods in our society. A number of literacy theorists (e.g., Gee, 1996; Luke, 1993) have posed that reading and writing practices—and people's valuing of these practices—are often tied to the race, social class, age, or gender of the readers and writers. Collins (1999) for example, illustrates in her study of one African American child in a middle school classroom, that the oral language practices (African American vernacular English) of the child and his family positioned them negatively in a conference about the boy's behavior in a classroom. Collins traces the child's experiences throughout school and shows how time and again he was positioned negatively through his reading, writing, and speaking practices. Consequently, we need to consider the politics of literacy—how is literacy used to make decisions about people's worth and potential? How is literacy used to shape people's worth and potential? How is literacy tied to race, class, gender, age, and other qualities of difference in our society?

Literacy in the Secondary School

Chemistry is more, I mean history, history is more facts, and um, just memorizing anyways. And chemistry, I mean, there's a lot of memorizing in it, but a lot of it is, a lot of the information you get varies, and there's a lot more to remember in chemistry.

Craig, 1993

Chemistry, you have never ever seen this before so if you don't study, then there is no way that you can get it. With English you can ask somebody what a five-page story is about, and they can tell you in one sentence and you just make up what you think it was.

Jay, 1993

It's [chemistry] not like English, where we have to find the hidden meanings.... I just like art classes because they teach us, like, new ways to, um, just like express ourselves on paper and stuff.

Heather, 1993

When I started teaching high school biology and history, I focused on delivering content concepts. I did not think about literacy except insofar as I gave assignments that depended on reading and writing. And I certainly did not think about how the literacy required in my classes might be different from the types of literacy required or valued in other content areas. After teaching and researching in secondary settings for a number of years, and especially after working with students like Craig, Jay, and Heather—students who saw clear differences in how knowledge was constructed and literacy enacted in different disciplines—I have learned that literate practice has a role in or an influence on every content area. Literacy in the content areas is shaped by the nature of the content area, as well as by the social context of the classroom and school. I have also learned that social contexts are complex and that they shape teaching and learning in profound ways.

For example, the structure of secondary schools in which students move from classroom to classroom promotes the development of multiple classroom cultures or subcultures. Within classrooms, teachers and students define and negotiate rules, norms, and values that create unique classroom cultures (Erickson, 1986; Mercer, 1992). Classroom cultures are defined by teachers' and students' (a) beliefs about the nature of knowledge; (b) philosophies and knowledge about the discipline, teaching and learning in that discipline, and teaching and learning in general; (c) past school experiences; (d) home and community experiences; and (e) feelings and emotions about school and about themselves in general. Teachers and students in secondary classrooms draw from these beliefs as they interact with one another. In their interactions with one another and with various texts, they construct meanings about literacy and learning events (Myers, 1992; Santa Barbara Discourse Group, 1994). The meaning that they make from their interaction shapes their future decisions about teaching and learning.

These beliefs, philosophies, experiences, and emotions also shape the socially acceptable forms of talking, reading, and writing in various disciplines or content areas. In this sense, literacy in secondary content classrooms is more than individual acts of reading, writing, and oral language. Embedded in secondary content area reading, writing, and oral language are beliefs and values about the appropriate uses of literacy within each discipline. It would seem unusual, for example, for students in a physics class to read a novel (although there are many wonderful novels that could be employed effectively in teaching physics), and it would seem equally odd for physical education students to learn how to play basketball by reading a book and writing about it. Students in an English literature class would not learn the *typical* habits of the discipline if they kept a log of the different readings they had done and then generated a theory of human interaction based on the "findings" in each log entry, even though such a practice might be fruitful for analyzing literature. Each of these acts are valid literacy acts, but they do not appear to fit well within the disciplinary practices that have been constructed by people over time.

Borrowing from the cross-cultural work that has posited that there are reading and writing practices unique to certain cultural groups (see, for example, Gee, 1996; Heath, 1983; Scribner & Cole, 1981; Street, 1984), we can argue that there are reading and writing practices unique to disciplinary groups, or to what Bizzell (1982) has called "discourse communities." What Bizzell means by this phrase is that there are groups of people who share common interests and perspectives and, as a result, engage in similar ways of reading, writing, and talking, hence the term "discourse." James Gee (1996) calls these ways of reading and writing (among other things), "Discourses," using the uppercase *D* to signify a distinction between discourse as a stretch of talk or language, and Discourse as a way of knowing, doing, believing, reading, or writing. It should not surprise us, however, to find that the practices or ways of knowing that are unique to a discipline are not always the same ones employed in classrooms that represent that discipline. Scientists, for example, engage in a great deal of very detailed journal (or log) writing, but extensive journal or log writing is rarely practiced in science classrooms.

Like Elliot Eisner (1994), I hope to shake up our notions of what it means to apply literacy in different disciplines—to illustrate that engaging with *multiple* forms of representation (such as conducting an experiment, keeping an investigation log, and reading a novel to learn biology) actually can lead to deeper understanding of ideas. Nevertheless, it is important to acknowledge that there are socially constructed practices unique to each discipline and to each school classroom, and those practices shape what is considered valid or acceptable literacy practice and resulting knowledge within the discipline and the classroom.

Reflection Point

Take some time to reflect on and jot in your journal some the literacy practices that are typical to your discipline. That is, how do scientists, mathematicians, sports figures or writers, historians, artists, musicians, linguists, literary authors, dancers, or dramatic performers read, write, and talk? Now that you've written down some of these practices, jot down the practices that you'd expect to see in your content area classroom. How are these practices similar? How are they different? What do you think accounts for some of the differences?

Remember that secondary teachers consider their primary job to be the teaching of content concepts. When I started teaching high school biology and history, I did not expect to teach students how to read and write biology and history. But I soon learned that teaching content concepts was much harder if students did not know how to read and write—at both basic and critical levels—in the discipline. I found myself teaching those skills despite my focus on content. And when I taught those skills, I found that the students learned the material more deeply and often became more engaged than they were when I practiced what Sizer calls the "pedagogy of telling" (Sizer, 1984). Thus, although I do not see every content area teacher as a "teacher of reading" (Herber, 1978), I do think it is important to recognize that literacy (reading and writing of written text) and its accompanying forms of representation (orality, performance, dance, art, and sign language) are used to make and represent knowledge in their content areas—whether in physics or physical education, mathematics or history, music or English—and these representational forms need to be taught in ways specific to their content area or discipline.

Another important point to keep in mind is that the secondary school is an institution. As O'Brien, Stewart, and Moje (1995) point out, the secondary school has its own set of norms that make it very different than the elementary school or the university. In the secondary school—whether middle, junior, or high school—as young people move from classroom to classroom, they are guided by bells, hall monitors and, in many urban settings, hall sweeps and lock downs. Astor, Meyer, and Behre (1999) and Eccles et al. (1993a) illustrate that control is the watchword of the secondary school, and controls are tightening because of recent incidents of school violence. High student-to-teacher ratios in secondary school classrooms (many teachers see as many as 180 different students each day) lend an impersonal air to secondary schools. And the competitive nature of both academic and extracurricular activities is heightened as the stakes become higher than they were at the elementary school level, with college scholarships and individual self-esteem often resting in the balance. (For more resources that address the nature of the secondary school, see Box 2-1.)

The Literacies in Adolescents' Lives In and Out of School

> *Well, Elizabeth, I guess I just wanted to be part of the story.*
>
> *Khek*

This quote was Khek's response to my question, "Why did you get so involved with gangs when you went to junior high school?" (For a detailed discussion of Khek's response, see Moje, in press). Khek's comment illustrates a common theme—the need to belong, to be part of something—that runs through the lives of adolescents. Adolescence is a time of development that is not particularly well understood. Stereotypes about the "storm and stress" (Hall, 1904) of adolescence suggest that youth struggle to deal with confusing hormonal changes that lead to erratic behavior. Current thinking on adolescence, however, argues that *contexts* may be as much a part of the unique behaviors and thoughts of adolescence as are changing hormones or physiology (see Connell, Spencer, & Aber, 1994; Connell & Wellborn, 1991). Several psychologists have shown, for example, that the secondary school setting itself—with its emphasis on control—may be responsible for many of the problems adolescents encounter in school and in society (e.g., Eccles, Lord, & Midgley, 1991; Eccles et al., 1993a). These scholars argue that many of the same developmental issues confronted in childhood and adulthood (especially middle adult-

BOX 2-1
Further Reading About the Secondary School Setting

If you're interested in reading more about the unique setting of the secondary school, you might want to consult some of the following materials:

Astor, R.A., Meyer, H.A., & Behre, W.J. (1999). Unowned places and times: Maps and interviews about violence in high schools. *American Educational Research Journal, 36*(1), 3–42.

Ball, S., & Lacey, C. (1984). Subject disciplines as the opportunity for a group action: A measured critique of subject sub-cultures. In A. Hargreaves & P. Woods (Eds.), *Classrooms and staffrooms: The sociology of teachers and teaching* (pp. 234–244). Milton Keynes, UK: Open University Press.

Eccles, J.S., Lord, S., & Midgley, C. (1991). What are we doing to early adolescents? The impact of educational contexts on early adolescents. *American Journal of Education, 99*(4), 521–542.

Eccles, J.S., & Midgley, C. (1989). Stage/environment fit: Developmentally appropriate classrooms for early adolescents. In R.E. Ames & C. Ames (Eds.), *Research on motivation in education* (Vol. 3, pp. 139–185). New York: Academic Press.

Eccles, J.S., Wigfield, A., Midgley, C., Reuman, D., MacIver, D., & Feldlaufer, H. (1993). Negative effects of traditional middle schools on students' motivation. *The Elementary School Journal, 93*, 553–574.

Lee, V.E., Bryk, A.S., & Smith, J.B. (1993). The organization of effective schools. In L. Darling-Hammond (Ed.), *Review of research in education* (Vol. 19, pp. 171–267). Washington, DC: American Educational Research Association.

Nieto, S. (1994). Lessons from students on creating a chance to dream. *Harvard Educational Review, 64*, 392–426.

O'Brien, D., Moje, E.B., & Stewart, R.A. (in press). Exploring the contexts of secondary and adolescent literacy: Literacy in people's everyday school lives. In E.B. Moje & D. O'Brien (Eds.), *Constructions of literacy: Studies of teaching and learning in and out of secondary schools*. Mahwah, NJ: Erlbaum.

O'Brien, D.G., Stewart, R.A., & Moje, E.B. (1995). Why content literacy is difficult to infuse into the secondary school: Complexities of curriculum, pedagogy, and school culture. *Reading Research Quarterly, 30*, 442–463.

Stodolsky, S.S., & Grossman, P. (1995). The impact of subject matter on curricular activity: An analysis of five academic subjects. *American Educational Research Journal, 32*(2), 227–249.

hood) are present in the lives of adolescents, but the contexts in which young people typically interact with adults shape those interactions in unique and complex ways. Especially important is the acknowledgment that although adolescents are often exhorted to "act responsibly," they are rarely given real responsibility, especially in secondary school settings. (For more readings on adolescence, see Box 2-2 on page 29.)

In this school context, in which they have little responsibility but many possibilities, youth use literacy practices to develop and maintain relationships and to make sense of an increasingly complicated world. Oates (in press) illustrates the ways in which adolescents use literacy to make a space for themselves in the world: He details how one young man he worked with wrote a letter objecting to the reading of *The House of the Spirits* (Allende, 1985)—a book he had never read that was listed as a reading option in a class he was not taking—as a way of achieving a prominent position in his church youth organization; this student's success in having the book removed from the class reading list ensured his identity as a committed and worthwhile member of the group. Thomas Bean and his daughters, Kristen and Shannon (Bean, Bean, & Bean, 1999), in their analysis of the two young women's everyday literacy practices, illustrate the different communicative practices in which adolescents engage on a daily basis. Bean et al. argue that adolescents have developed sociotechnical forms of literacy, but that adult teachers rarely address such forms in our secondary school classrooms.

The gang-connected young people with whom I worked over the last 3 years used similar—and yet very different—literacy practices as a way of constructing and maintaining identities. These practices, however, important as they are to youth, are usually not valued by adults. In fact, they are often vilified. An excerpt of an interview I had with Chile illustrates how she felt about the literacy practices in which she and her siblings engaged:

Chile: Like some of my friends and stuff, like the poems that I've, or that they write and stuff, I mean, I could show you some of the poems that they, like that my sister has and stuff. And that her friends have written her and my friends have written. And it's like, "Somethin' from my set and this and this and this. And all my homies are there, na na na." You know, and they write really good. And you know, they write good things like…I don't know, they make up like, they'll sit there and they'll make up like all this stuff…they'll like make up little things and stuff. But at least they're like, you know, they're clever 'cause they can make up like little things. Every time, like my friend would write me, you know, she's like, I don't know, she's like, "Let it rain, let it flood, oh, let it rain, let it flood, let a Crip kill a Blood," or somethin' like that. And she'd write little, she'd write little poems, and then, like my friends would write long poems and stuff, and it was so pretty and stuff. And my sister, she wrote her, but they never appreciate it,

---

BOX 2-2
Further Reading About the Sociocultural Contexts of Adolescence

For more on adolescence as a complex construct of the individual and the social and cultural setting (especially schools), consult the following readings:

Connell, J.P. , Spencer, M.B., & Aber, J.L. (1994). Educational risk and resilience in African American youth: Context, self, and action outcomes in school. *Child Development, 65,* 493–506.

Connell, J.P., & Wellborn, J.G. (1991). Competence, autonomy, and relatedness: A motivational analysis of self-system processes. In R. Gunnar & L.A. Sroufe (Eds.), *Minnesota symposia on child psychology* (Vol. 23, pp. 43–77). Hillsdale, NJ: Erlbaum.

Eccles, J.S., Adler, T.F., Futterman, R., Goff, S.B., Kaczala, C.M., Meece, J.L., & Midgley, C. (1983). Expectancies, values, and academic behaviors. In J.T. Spence (Ed.), *Achievement and achievement motivation* (pp. 75–146). San Francisco: W.H. Freedman.

Eccles, J.S., Midgley, C., Wigfield, A., Miller-Buchanan, C., Reuman, D., Flanagan, C., & MacIver, D. (1993a). Development during adolescence: the impact of stage-environment fit on young adolescents' experiences in schools and families. *American Psychologist, 48,* 90–101.

Eckert, P. (1989). *Jocks and burnouts: Social categories and identity in the high school.* New York: Teachers College Press.

Everhart, R. (1983). *Reading, writing, and resistance: Adolescence and labor in a junior high school.* Boston: Routledge and Kegan Paul.

Fairbanks, C.M. (1998). Nourishing conversations: Urban adolescents, literacy, and democratic society. *Journal of Literacy Research, 30,* 187–203.

Farrell, E.W. (1990). *Hanging in and dropping out: Voices of at-risk high school students.* New York: Teachers College Press.

Farrell, E.W. (1994). *Self and school success: Voices and lore of inner-city students.* Albany, NY: State University of New York Press.

Finders, M. (1997). *Just girls.* New York: Teachers College Press; Urbana, IL: National Council of Teachers of English.

Finders, M.J. (1998/1999). Raging hormones: Stories of adolescence and implications for teacher preparation. *Journal of Adolescent & Adult Literacy, 42,* 252–263.

>you know, teachers read poems like that, read'em and they'd be like, "Give me that," and things like that.

Elizabeth: The teachers?

Chile: Yeah. And, and like my bro, my sis, my whole, my sister wrote a big long poem. And like, I remember it, it was so pretty, it was, I memorized it 'cause I helped her write some of it. And it was just really pretty 'cause it was for her boyfriend and stuff. And then he wrote, he wrote her one too. And they'd just like write poems back and forth.

Complicated dress codes; gang signs; and "tagging up" (writing graffiti on) books, desks, and bodies were all literacy practices that identified certain youth as members of particular groups. Literacy practices allow kids to construct and be part of life stories (see also Camitta, 1993; Finders, 1996). These practices also allowed teens to construct identities in relation to various groups—to become part of larger, unfolding stories around them.

Literacy as More Than Print: Multiple Forms of Representation

Chile: And there's Danielle…. She's always throwin' up [flashing a hand sign] Westside too but—

Elizabeth: Oh, is that what that means?

Chile: Yeah.

Elizabeth: Wait, show me.

Chile: There's the *W* and then there's, she has *W* right here too. And that was James and some other dude in the background, they were flippin' em off.

Elizabeth: So it's like this?

Chile: Like this. Just put your middle finger over your ring finger…. Because we were like, we did it 'cause we wanted it to be like that thing where you go like this [a flip book], you know, we stood still and we went like this and then we go like this, like this, like this. We did all Westside and then when you went through it [the stack of pictures]—

Elizabeth: Like, like a movie.

Chile: Yeah, we were doin' it all fast, it was funny….

Studying the literacy practices of gang-connected adolescents has challenged me to think about all the different ways that people make meaning, represent and communicate understandings and beliefs, and express themselves. The hand signs to which Chile refers also constitute a symbol system that is used to make meaning. In that sense, these hand signs are an aspect of literate practice because, although they are not encoded in permanent form (written text), they are communicative practices (see Street, 1995) and can be used to make sense of or to extend written text.

What's more, many other forms of representation (for example, a dance that is performed or an oral speech) shape the meanings that we make from our interpretations of written text. In other words, oral and visual representations shape literate, that is, written representations. We can help our adolescent students learn the many symbol systems and signs that are used to make and represent meaning in addition to written language (Eisner, 1994; New London Group, 1996). I talk about these multiple forms (such as orality, performance, or artistic representations) as part of the young people's literacy practices. Literacy, even when defined solely as the reading and writing of print, cannot be well understood or taught unless one attends to people's literacy practices and to the multiple symbol systems and signs to which reading and writing of print are connected.

Responsive and "Planful" Teaching

> It gives you a really happy feeling to know that maybe in some little way, you may have some influence on what they're [students] going to do with their lives. And it may not be with the chemistry, but maybe something that you said, a word of encouragement, maybe a skill you've taught them.... I've got the sense, intuitive sense of what I believe is good for kids. I look at myself and say, "Would this be something that I'd like to be experiencing?" And if I say no, I certainly wouldn't give it them.... I guess I look at each student the way he or she comes. I say, "How can I reach that student?" I think there's a special creativity in each person. And you have to know which button to hit. Once the creativity's out there, you [the student] do more and more. It makes you [the student] feel good, because you get told "That was a really good job." And it has to permeate any kind of teaching you do.
>
> Landy

A primary aspect of my philosophy of literacy teaching and learning is a commitment to responsive teaching. Responsive teaching, for me, is different from child-centered education, although responsive teaching certainly puts the child or adolescent in the foreground of the educational process. Child-centered teaching, however, often revolves around the idea that we must follow students and give them complete choice in their learning if they are to be engaged. Such a stance rarely challenges students to move beyond their own, individual experiences toward an awareness of how they are part of a larger social system. With a focus on the individual, child-centered pedagogies often fail to account for socially structured differences, such as differences in race, class, gender, and age. As a result, child-centered pedagogies, as Thompson (1998) argues, are often blind to how difference shapes students' ways of knowing and being, as well as to how certain structures in society privilege some ways of knowing and devalue others. What's more, child-centered pedagogy, as traditionally conceived, is derived from ways of knowing that put the individual at center stage and focus on developing self, rather than developing community or group (Dressman, 1993).

Responsive teaching, by contrast, makes the learners' experiences central to the learning process and acknowledges that teachers, as adults who have particular kinds of expertise and experience in the world, have the ethical responsibility not only to draw from adolescents' experiences but also to extend and challenge them. Responsive teaching starts where kids are, but also pushes them to new understandings, experiences, and awareness. Responsive teaching also assumes that there are many different ways of knowing the world and that students have the right to gain access to these many different ways of knowing.

This extending, challenging, and pushing, however, does not take place according to a prescribed curriculum or set of standards, nor is it based only in what the teacher wants from or believes about the world. Some important criticisms have been made of simple admonitions to teachers to "care" about their students (Pratt, 1991; Thompson, 1997). If teachers are to avoid discriminatory practice, then an ethic of care must be based on more than asking oneself, "Would I like to be experiencing this?" although that's a useful initial question. Because students come from many different backgrounds and have different kinds of knowledge and experiences, responsive teachers learn about their students' lives and make decisions about the learning experiences that would best meet each young person's needs. Responsive teachers acknowledge other ways of knowing and the many "funds of knowledge" (Moll, Veléz-Ibañéz, & Greenberg, 1989)—or family and cultural knowledge bases—that young people bring to school. (For more on funds of knowledge, see Chapter 3 and Box 3-1 on page 41.) Drawing from multiple ways of knowing and funds of knowledge, including their own, responsive teachers construct *planful* pedagogy. That is, they construct pedagogy that begins with concepts and skills important to students' lives and that connects concepts to each other in coherent, systematic, and thoughtful ways.

Being "planful" is different from engaging in planning. Planning suggests simply making lists of activities and times, perhaps connecting the activities to learning objectives. But planfulness is a quality of teaching in which teachers make decisions about learning activities with their students' needs, knowledge, larger learning goals, and beliefs in mind. (I discuss planful teaching in more detail in Chapter 6.) Responsive and planful teachers, in the words of Ms. Landy, look at each student "the way he or she comes" and ask, "How am I going to reach this student?" and "Toward what end?"

A Cautionary Note

In the remainder of the book I present voices of young people, unedited (except to achieve clarity). If you are like me, you will find many of these voices discouraging. In fact, I had not realized how discouraging some of the youths' comments were until I began to systematically analyze the patterns in comments of kids from many different studies that I had conducted. I realized in this cross-case analysis that both successful and struggling students, both mainstream and marginalized, have negative things to say about their school experiences. As I wrote the first drafts of this book, I worried that readers would be so dismayed that they would not want to continue. But as I finished the book I realized that there is much that we can learn from these comments, even when the comments are not ones we like to hear. Consequently, I want to caution and encourage you before you read on: What you are about to read may seem discouraging and almost hopeless, but when you read the voices of young people who are engaged in generative learning experiences and who are working with teachers who communicate an ethic of care and respect for students, I believe that you will be encouraged. You will see that adolescents have many insights—both negative and positive—about education, and that these insights can help educators rethink and restructure practice.

It may be easy to dismiss these stories as coming from the voices of a few young people, or to wonder if they were just telling me what they thought I wanted to hear. On that note, keep in mind that I worked intensively with most of these young people for extensive time periods, ranging anywhere from a school semester (4 months) to 4 years. I have also been careful to choose representative, not merely titillating, insights from the youth. In addition, if you are questioning the usefulness of these research stories, I encourage you to note the *patterns* in the insights. Although I would never generalize from one young person's stories to all young people, I am compelled by the patterns in kids' stories and insights across my studies (and across the research of others) to argue for some generalizability in these stories.

In the next chapter, I use insights drawn from my interactions with one young woman, Chile, to discuss ways to learn about adolescent students' funds of knowledge and literacy practices—what they know, care about, can do well, and need to learn.

Chapter 3

"All the Stories That We Have": Kids' Insights About Literacy

It's writing time in third-period English class. The seventh-graders are working on various tasks in their writing workshop, some drafting new pieces, some conferring or revising already drafted pieces. Some, like Chile, are thinking about what to write next. After staring into space for a minute, Chile moves to the desk next to Elizabeth, who is finishing her notes on the status of the class. With her long, straight, black hair draped over her face, Chile leans over to Elizabeth and says, "Guess what, my aunt died yesterday. She was, like, 100." Instead of writing, Chile tells the story of Tia Lola, which is, ultimately, a story of Chile, her family, and her literacy practices. The story of Tia Lola becomes the story of her abuela (grandmother), Sofia, which suddenly, sublimely, becomes the Mexican folktale of la Llorona (the weeping woman): They would "always talk about the Llorona," Chile says, as she launches into the tale for Elizabeth, who has never heard this story before. Before Elizabeth realizes it, 20 minutes have passed, and now Shel Silverstein and Chile's nephew, Ryan, have become part of the tale.

Why do I tell this story of Chile to begin the chapter on kids' insights about literacy and language? I sat in this classroom, enraptured, listening to Chile spin the tale of *la Llorona*, all the while thinking that Chile should be writing—it was writing time, after all. Even as I thought that, though, I found myself wondering why Chile needed to write when these oral stories had survived so well and were, through Chile and her family, being constantly reinvented.

Nevertheless, I began to feel anxious as I saw and felt my teaching and research colleague, Diane (the classroom teacher) looking over from time to time. I could tell that Diane was wondering why I was spending so much time with one student and why that student was talking rather than writing. Diane believed that students need to spend time writing in order to learn to write well. Her thinking made obvious sense, and yet, as I talked to Chile, my commitment to building connections between oral and written language, between out-of-school and in-school literacy practices, deepened: Don't people write more, and write better, if they spend time talking to each other, and if writing is not privileged as the primary communicative practice in the classroom? As I struggled with these questions, I turned back to Chile and, feeling foolish, told Chile that she should consider writing some of these stories down as a family collection so that the stories would continue to be told. Fortunately, Chile ignored my exhortation to write and went on to tell how these stories play a part in her everyday life:

> Chile: We would tell my, my um, my nephew about gypsies, and we were telling him they'd take him.
>
> Elizabeth: So you tell your nephew, you don't tell about *la Llorona*, you tell about...
>
> Chile: Yeah, I tell, I tell him about the, I told him *la Llorona* [will get him] because um, he's bad. I told him, I go, "Guess who I saw?" and he's all, "Oh no! *La Llorona*, did she take you, did she kill you?" I go, I go, "Yeah, and then she brought me back to life." (Laughs.) And then he's like, he's all, "My gosh."…And, and like, there's like this fortune teller, this fortune telling place, you know, by the, by the body piercing store, um, we, we would drive past her when we were goin' to the movies. I go, "Ryan, lookit, there's the gypsy lady." That was the lady sitting there, you know, and then he goes, "Where's the gypsy?" Then I'd knock on the door and I go, I go, "Oh, the gypsy's here." And I'd tell him that, you know, the, the *Where the Sidewalk Ends* [Silverstein, "Kids for Sale," 1974], that book, it goes, "Gypsies are coming," and, "Ten cents for fat ones,

eleven cents for skinny ones." No, it says, "And just between you and me they never take the *bad* ones."…And
I, but I, but instead I go, "But just between you and me
they never take the *good* ones," and then, so he's like always nice and everything 'cause he's afraid to be bad.

At that point another student approached. This time I was firm with Chile.
I told her that these were great stories and they would be great material
for her writer's notebook. "Write some of this down," I urged, and then I
left her so that I could work with the other student. When I looked in
Chile's notebook later, I was dismayed to find that Chile had not written
anything, let alone the wonderful tales of *la Llorona*, her family, and "Kids
for Sale."

Reflection Point

Write in your journal about what would you have done if you
were Chile's teacher—in any content area—and she began to
tell you these stories when she was supposed to be engaged in
an assignment you had given. In what ways might you bring these
stories into the curriculum? What, if anything, would you encourage her to do with these experiences?

As Chile told me how she wove the *la Llorona* tale together with Shel
Silverstein's poetry to construct an intertext—that is, a text that makes use
of and speaks to many other texts—during an everyday interaction with
her nephew, I marveled at her sophistication, her ability to make stories
a part of her everyday life and to use them to explain events or to shape
situations. In conversations over the next 2 years, Chile again and again
revealed her love of stories and her knowledge of the world. On one occasion she told me that she was excited about the Greek mythology she
was about to study in school; she then told me one myth after another,
in exacting detail. I asked her how she knew so much about Greek
mythology, expecting to hear that she watched a popular fantasy

television show about the Greek gods and goddesses. Instead, Chile told me that her sisters have told her the myths throughout her childhood. Hearing her answer, I sat open-mouthed, while images of Chile's sisters, two of them former gangsters, telling stories to little Chile danced before me. When I expressed my surprise, Chile explained that her whole family loves stories, and not just the telling of stories:

> My mom, she's always saying, "Write a story, Write a story." And my mom wanted to write, she goes, "Do you know what?" She goes, "I think that if we try," she goes, "I think that we could write a book." 'Cause she wanted to, she goes, she goes, "I think that it would be so nice because of all the stories that we have," of how, um, like of, what's it called, um, she was like, she was sayin' that the title was like, "*Tierra de Mi Sangre*," it's "The Land of my Blood."

It is clear from her mother's words that Chile wrote outside of school. In addition to the stories that she spoke of, Chile kept a journal and wrote in it regularly. When I presented Chile with a writing journal as a Christmas gift, she thanked me profusely—exhibiting much more enthusiasm than she had when I had given her earrings on her birthday. On one occasion when I was with Chile and Khek, Chile got into my car and handed Khek a three-page letter that she had written to Khek, obviously valuing the written word as a way of communicating about a private matter between them.

In another interview, I listened to Chile recite poems that her friend had written; some were poems with a street gang theme (see Moje, in press) and some were love poems. I was stunned when, after asking Chile if she would write them down for me, she immediately pulled a notebook out of her backpack to show me that she had already written them. She carried these poems and other writings that she liked with her every day.

Reading was also important to Chile. In addition to the more mainstream adolescent novels that she read (*The Giver* [Lowry, 1993] was her favorite), Chile read informational text about events that were an important part of her life. In this interview excerpt, Chile tells of a trip to the library to examine some news documents that reported on gang violence:

Oh, and I got this thing from the library, it was a, it was a Salt Lake um, police thing. It had a time line from 1994 to '95 or something like that. Of all the gang activity. They had the wrong day that um, the wrong day that my friends died, it was the wrong date. The time of [cousin's name] arrest, my cousin's name was in there, [cousin's name] was arrested for the shooting of [another gangster's name] on this day and it was a Cinco de Mayo thing.

Finally, in several different interviews across my 3 years of working with Chile, she recounted stories from novels and movies that she had seen, describing them all in exacting detail. In one interview, for example, Chile provided me with seven pages of interview transcript that described the movie, *Bound by Honor* (1993), a movie about Chicano gang wars in the California prison system. She also repeatedly described scenes from *Always Running: La Vida Loca: Gang Days in L.A.*, a novel by Luis Rodriguez (1993) about his life in and exit from gangs, as well as several other novels about gang life. Chile was obviously a reader of both traditional print forms and many other forms of representation in the world.

Chile's experiences with language and literacy in and out of school compel us to rethink our assumptions about who kids are as language and literacy learners and about what they want to experience in literacy and language education. It was clear to me from my 3 years of intense interaction with Chile that literacy was a critical part of her everyday life, yet *virtually all of these literate practices occurred outside of school*. The stories she wrote for her writer's workshop class were amusing and skillful, but they did not weave together the life stories that she told and wrote about or the novels and movies that she represented to me. Furthermore, despite Chile's love of language and of story, despite her proficiency at spinning a tale—both orally and in writing—Chile began to struggle in school by the end of her seventh-grade year. Why? What was missing in Chile's school-based education that led to her lack of engagement, her frequent absence from classes, her apathy for learning? What can Chile teach us about how to teach literacy, not only in a secondary school English classroom, but also in the various content areas of the secondary school?

*Reflection Point*_____

Does Chile remind you of any of your own students? In the introductory Kids InSight book, *Kids InSight: Reconsidering How to Meet the Literacy Needs of All Students*, Deborah Dillon writes about *responsive teaching*, which reflects the idea that as teachers we need to teach to the needs and interests of students rather than to a standard curriculum. How do you think you could be responsive to the needs of a student like Chile? Choose one of your own students to study for one week. What can you learn about this student's "funds of knowledge," or the things he or she knows about the world before he or she even comes to your class? How will you learn about these funds of knowledge? How will you be responsive in the classroom to this student's needs? (For further discussion of the term "funds of knowledge," see Box 3-1.)

What Chile and Other Kids Can Teach Us

Chile's story highlights the importance of learning about who young people are and what they know, or their "funds of knowledge" outside of school. Chile, for example, knew a great deal about story, particularly folk story. She has a rich resource of oral stories, complete with the skill to tell a good story and to weave it together with other oral and written stories to create a sophisticated intertext. Like Chile, several other youth with whom I have worked had important funds of knowledge and engaged in rich literacy practices outside of school. For example, in one conversation, Jeffrey told me about how the Aztec Indians in what is now Mexico were massacred or colonized by the Spanish, explaining that he had learned these stories not in school but from his grandfather:

> **Jeffrey:**   It's like Aztec, Aztecs were Indians but now they're like, now they're like Mexican.
>
> **Elizabeth:** Have you ever had classes about the Aztecs in school? (He shakes his head no.) You never had anything where you

> ## BOX 3-1
> ## Funds of Knowledge
> The phrase "funds of knowledge" comes from the work of Luis Moll and his colleagues, who used the phase in their work as they engaged elementary school teachers in the process of learning about the cultural practices and knowledges available to students in their homes and communities (see Moll 1994; Moll, Veléz-Ibañez, & Greenberg, 1989; Moll & Whitmore, 1993). Moll and his colleagues supported teachers in conducting community and family ethnographies to help them learn about the rich resources students had in their homes and to help teachers find ways to bring these funds of knowledge into the classroom. Similarly, Shirley Brice Heath (1983) studied the "ways with words" of children in three communities and used her work to facilitate teachers' research in the communities in which they taught. Other excellent resources for learning about students' literacy practices outside of school include Camitta, 1993; Finders, 1996; Moje, in press; and Shuman, 1986.

talked about the Aztecs? You're kidding. The Mayans, any of that? That's a shame, 'cause that's your ancestry.

Jeffrey: See 'cause like, the Aztecs, they live in Mexico and the white man, they came with like guns and they killed them all for their gold, 'cause there was a lot of gold, like everybody wore like gold hats and gold earrings in their noses and bracelets and stuff like that. And, the white man came on the boat and they found where they lived, like their villages, and they killed them all and they just took their gold 'cause it was worth a lot of money. But it still wasn't, it still wasn't worth a lot of money back then 'cause they didn't really know. But they liked it for the show and because it was flashy.

Elizabeth: Right, it looked really pretty...so where, since you didn't learn about that in school, where did you learn those stories? From your family?

Jeffrey: Yeah, my grandpa tells me a lot about like, his mom and stuff.

Similarly, Heather, who was a high academic achiever in most classes but was apathetic about school learning, revealed to me in several different conversations that she read widely outside of school. She read the philosopher Nietzsche, for example, because his ideas "seemed interesting"

(Dillon & Moje, 1998), and she asked herself many questions about the chemistry concepts she was learning in conjunction with these outside readings. In one interview, she linked Nietzsche's questioning of truth to the study of nuclear chemistry: "How do we know that this table is composed of atoms? How do we know that it's true? It's all just theory. I guess I'm just a doubting Thomas." During the entire year that I observed daily in her classroom, however, she did not ask any of those questions. As she said, "I'm just not that kind of student." As a result, Heather became invisible in her chemistry class, even though her teacher, Ms. Landy, cared deeply about supporting young women's pursuits of science as a career.

This information about students' funds of knowledge and literacy practices is important in two ways. First, such information can provide teachers with a resource for building a curriculum that incorporates what students already know and can do. Instead of assessing students' prior knowledge about particular, teacher-determined topics via a K-W-L strategy (Ogle, 1986), for example, teachers might consider also spending time with students (as individuals or in groups) to learn who they are and what they know. Thus, a strategy such as K-W-L could be used to refine and focus the inquiry that young people do in classrooms, but such a strategy should not be the only means of getting to know students' prior knowledge, experiences, and stories.

In addition, information about students' funds of knowledge can challenge our assumptions about youth. Chile, Heather, and Jeffrey were all at the margins in different ways in their school experience (although Heather made high grades in most of her classes), in part because their teachers did not have access to certain insights about who they were as people outside of the classroom. For example, because Heather did not say much in class, Landy did not know of the deep and thoughtful questions that Heather asked herself when she did her homework. I have always thought it interesting that Heather was not recommended for honors chemistry, even though she received high grades in chemistry, but another young woman who was much more vocal during class was recommended to move to honors chemistry. Their grades seemed equivalent, but Landy felt that the other young woman had more drive and ambition. If Landy had known about what Heather was reading outside of school, she might have seen Heather in a different light. Landy might have pushed Heather more and might have encouraged her in a way that would have brought those unspoken questions to voice. Thus, learning about the literacy practices in which youth engage out of school can help teachers draw from those practices and extend them even further.

Second, this information reveals something especially important if one is using a teaching approach in which young people are asked to write about or research their experiences as the basis of study in a content area. The premise of most literacy workshop approaches, for example, is that students will be able to express themselves more fully if they write from their experiences (see Atwell, 1987). Self-expression is thought to be both a way to support fluency in writing and an important aspect of the learning that children do. Chile, however, wrote dutifully in the writer's workshop that Diane had set up, but she did not write about the kinds of experiences and cultural knowledges that she had shared with me. Like many other students I worked with, and like students in other classrooms (see Fassio, 1999; Lensmire, 1994; Willis, 1995), Chile wrote what she considered appropriate stories for the English classroom, using a form of writing (genre) or way of writing (what Gee [1996] calls a "Discourse") that seemed to fit the accepted genre and Discourse of the class.

This resistance to sharing "authentic" experiences poses a critical problem for experience-based approaches such as the writer's workshop. If students believe, for whatever reason, that they cannot write, talk, or read about their actual experiences, then the pedagogy is not really doing what it is supposed to do. Knowing students' backgrounds and experiences will allow teachers to challenge this fairly typical practice among students. For example, as Diane and I became aware of this pattern in students' writing, we realized that we were modeling only certain genres of writing, and thus we were setting the norms for socially acceptable topics, Discourses, and genres. We changed the nature of the writer's workshop as a result. Similarly, when Kris Fassio and her teaching colleague, Ruth, who taught in a second-grade classroom, found their students making up stories in order to look good for their peers, they revised their pedagogy to engage the students in discussions and writing about their exaggerations and deceptions (see Fassio, 1999). And in her book *On the Brink: Negotiating Literature and Life With Adolescents*, Hynds (1997) illustrates that when a teacher knows something about her students, she can build relationships with them that encourage writing about actual experiences.

Finally, such information lets teachers know what they do *not* need to concentrate on with particular students and with groups of students. Chile, for example, does not need to learn how to tell a good story. She is already proficient at that. As Delpit (1988) has argued, many adolescents are already fluent and creative; they do not need a writer's workshop to practice such skills. They may, instead, need to focus on the form or correctness of their writing, or they may need to learn particular content concepts and skills such as framing research questions or synthesizing information across texts. For instance, although Chile could weave two or more stories together with skill, she was not as skilled at pulling together information in a ninth-grade geography class research project in which she was to study one country and create a portfolio of information about it. In fact, she failed that year-long assignment and had to retake her geography class during summer school. Instead of focusing solely on writing expressive or narrative stories in her English class, perhaps Chile should have been guided in research and reporting skills. Or, Chile's English and geography teachers could have worked together on a cross-disciplinary project in which these skills were taught in a team approach. Gaining knowledge about students' out-of-school practices can help teachers design teaching that meets the specific needs of many different kinds of learners. The goal, of course, is not to design 150 to 180 different units of study based on individual kids' interests and needs. The goal is to design a palette of practices, skills, and strategies to be woven into a responsive and planful teaching curriculum.

Moreover, it is important to note that the writer's workshop approach in which we focused on personal, expressive, and narrative writing did not hold Chile's (and other students') attention throughout the year, suggesting the need for a more varied curriculum plan, one that expands students' horizons even as it builds on their experiences and interests. Chile became apathetic about her writing, often searching for topics to write about, even though she had a rich resource of experiences (many of which she felt were inappropriate for school writing). By the end of her seventh-grade year, Chile skipped the English class and other classes often. During eighth grade, Chile racked up quite a truancy record. When I asked her why she missed so much school, she responded that it just wasn't interesting; Chile saw little purpose in her school learning. This lack of purpose is not solely the fault of the literacy workshop; her other classes did even less to tap her interests and her existing funds of knowledge. It is important to keep in mind that knowing what kids do well and what they have not had much experience with can help teachers plan interesting, engaging, and educative experiences for students, rather than simply offering them a set pedagogy that is deemed "best practice" for a particular content area.

Reflection Point

What does your teaching currently look like? Try drawing a picture of what your teaching looks like. Do your students use their experiences to help them learn the content of your class? Do you use their experiences as part of your teaching curriculum? What do you do to find out about their experiences? What more could you do to learn about the funds of knowledge the students bring to your classroom?

Chapter 4

Bringing Kids' Stories Into Sight: Ideas for Getting and Keeping Students in Our Sights

It seems clear from observations of Chile that we need to know more about our students' lives and experiences outside of school if we are to help them be successful in school. Yet, one of the most challenging aspects of such responsive teaching—especially at the secondary school level, in which we can easily find ourselves teaching between 150 to 180 students each day—is figuring out who young people are and what they want. Specifically, what is it that we should respond to? Good teachers know how important it is to find out what is going on in students' lives, both in terms of literacy learning and social well being. Recent incidents of school violence involving disenfranchised and troubled youth underscore the importance of learning about young people outside of our classrooms. But how do we learn who our students are when our professional and personal time is so limited?

"Kickin' It" With Kids

One way to find out about who young people are is to spend time with them outside the classroom. I make this suggestion fully recognizing that our lives as teachers are busy and complex, and that teachers simply cannot "hang out" with young people the way I could as a researcher. That said, I offer the following anecdote as an example of one way to learn more about students and to underscore the importance of such learning.

Toward the end of our year together in a writer's workshop class-room, Diane, the seventh grade writing workshop teacher, and I attended a performance of an African American dance and drum troupe in which two of our students appeared. During the performance we closely watched one of the drummers, Mark, one of Diane's students who was considered to be hyperactive and disengaged from school. Mark performed with intense concentration throughout the entire event. We were surprised by his ability not only to attend to the lead drummer, but to maintain such intense and calm concentration. So many descriptions of Mark positioned him as a problem, but our out-of-school observations challenged us to rethink our understanding of this young man. Was something in the curriculum or school contributing to his inattention in class? Could the curriculum's lack of cultural and racial diversity have played a part in his lack of engagement? Upon returning to school we looked through his writer's notebook and found an abandoned piece on African drumming. We began to look at our pedagogy and pondered why Mark had abandoned this work about experiences that were obviously interesting and important to him. What in our pedagogy did not encourage him to move forward with the piece? What could we do to encourage him in the future? Not only did our thinking about Mark and the curriculum change as a result of this out-of-school experience, but our interactions with Mark also changed. Perhaps this change occurred because Mark felt more connected to us once we had become a part of his life outside of school, or perhaps it occurred because we were more willing to see Mark in a different way.

As you will note, Diane and I did not have to spend months, weeks, or even days with Mark outside of school to learn something important about him, something that we could use to draw him into writing and to shape the curriculum we offered students. From one 3-hour evening—an enjoyable one, I should add—we learned something that reshaped our teaching (and research) for all the students in the class. As a result, I have made it my policy as a teacher, even as a teacher of teachers, to try to spend some time with a small number of students outside the classroom. If I were teaching middle, junior, or high school now, I would identify at least 10 students who could serve as touchstones, or representatives of, the other students. Chances are that if I were to eat lunch occasionally with these 10 students, attend special events in which they were partici-pating, and even visit their homes one time each, I would probably end up spending time with other students as well. For example, Chile and Khek routinely brought along friends on our outings, and Anthony and Jeffrey each brought friends with them on at least one occasion; when Heather and I got together outside of school, her mother dropped her off, giving me the chance to chat with Heather's mother for a short time. Each in-teraction with young people and the significant people in their lives will provide a wealth of information about the practices, beliefs, values, and knowledges that they bring to the classroom.

Reflection Point

To experiment "kickin' it" with students, choose a student who puzzles you or one with whom you've struggled a bit this year. Arrange to meet with the student outside of school (with parents' permission, of course). You might ask to visit them at home or you might attend an event that is not sponsored by the school (a church or community event, for example). As soon as possible af-ter the meeting or event, record your observations of the student and the context in which you observed. Then a day or two later, interview the student, asking questions about the event. Ana-lyze your observations and the interview responses in regard to the different ways you saw the youth using literacy. Use the ques-tions in Box 4-1 to guide your analysis.

Let me give an example of how I might analyze an out-of-school ob-servation in ways that would shape my literacy teaching, in any content area. Consider my experience with Mark. As suggested in Box 4-1, I asked myself about the literacies that were evident in Mark's performance. I would start by focusing on the ways in which Mark's practices were like school literacy practices: First, Mark followed a written program that cued him into when he would perform and for how long. Second, he followed

> ## BOX 4-1
> ### Possible Observation Foci
> - What school-like literacy practices stood out in your observation of a particular student?
> - What other kinds of literacies did the adolescent or others around him or her make use of?
> - Did you observe anything about the student that surprised you? Write about what you saw and reflect on how such knowledge might influence your teaching.
> - Did you observe any practices that you might bring into your teaching? Don't limit this to literacy practices. Are there interests in music, movies, or social activities that you could build on?

written, spoken, and "drummed" directions prior to and during his performance. Third, Mark worked in a group to achieve a specific goal. Each of these practices is very much like what one might see successful students doing in school.

Other literacy practices were also evident in Mark's performance (see the second question in Box 4-1). (Keep in mind that literacy *practices* include all forms of representation that a person uses to make meaning.) Mark and his fellow drummers communicated with each other and with the dancers that they accompanied. They communicated not only when and how to move or how to drum through their various rhythms, but they also communicated aspects of their cultural heritage, because drumming and dancing are significant representational and communicative forms in African and African American cultures (Kelly, in press). Through their literacy practices of drumming and dancing, they established and maintained identities and relationships.

Next, I asked myself what surprised me about Mark's practices (see the third question in Box 4-1). As I have already indicated, both Diane and I were amazed by Mark's concentration and attention to his task. In addition, he cooperated with the other drummers and followed his drum leader closely—something we had not observed him doing in our classroom. These observations led us to question ourselves and our practices.

Finally, I thought about ways that I could bring these practices—both the nonmainstream literacy practices and their accompanying ways of being (concentration, cooperation, attention)—into whatever class I was teaching. In an English or social studies classroom, for example, I would ask Mark to demonstrate African drumming for the class and to teach the class its significance in African and African American cultures. In the English classroom (or any class that focuses on language and discourse), I might use the drumming as a springboard to engage students in a larger unit of focused inquiry about many different forms of representation and communication—dance, art, music, and video. This would allow me to invite forms of representation valued by other students into the classroom. We would examine how meaning making from these forms compares to meaning making from print forms, engaging in analyses of what meanings are gained and lost when understanding is represented through one form versus another (for more on the different kinds of cognition possible via different forms of representation, see Eisner, 1994). In the social studies classroom, I might ask students to engage in inquiry about how different forms of representation have come to be valued differently over time. We could examine how time, geography, economics, and politics shape the ways that people communicate and how such communication is valued. Further, in a mathematics classroom, we could examine the rhythms of both the drum and dance as mathematical systems and perhaps try to translate other mathematical forms into the rhythms of drum and dance. In physical education, music, dance, drama, or visual arts, we could practice the drumming and dancing or render them in other forms (sculpture, painting, drawing, and music). Imagine the rich potential for weaving the study of African drumming and dance and related concepts across disciplines and into other content concepts—teams of students and teachers could take these inquiries in many different directions, all prompted by one evening of entertainment in which a student performed the literacy practices that play a key role in his everyday life.

Interviewing Individuals and Groups

Another way to learn more about students is to conduct informal interviews with them. It is obviously not practical to conduct interviews with all of the students one might have as a secondary teacher, but I have found, much like Tom Nicholson did, (see Nicholson, 1984) that interviewing even 10 students a year can provide important information,

information that can challenge assumptions we often make as teachers. To include the voices of more youth within a reasonable time frame, I also engage small groups of students in "focus group" interviews. Focus groups can be useful because participants can listen to the perspectives of others and bounce ideas off one another. Focus groups can also be excellent learning tools, so that you can teach while also getting a sense of what your students' interests are. However, focus groups need to be supplemented by individual interviews, because some youth will not talk in front of others and because some will try to impress others in the group by making humorous comments or by embellishing on their own experiences.

Individual and group interviewing can be especially helpful if one chooses interviewees carefully. I select young people to interview based on participation levels in class, types of writing or reading that students do, and interaction patterns (such as students who do not speak much, students who speak all the time, students who fight). I also make sure to choose a number of female and male students that represents the larger group from which I am drawing, and I choose members of different ethnic and social class groups. When I meet with youth, I ask them straightforward questions, keeping in mind that I may need to repeat the questions in subsequent conversations because their answers will change as our relationship changes. Following is an excerpt of an individual interview I conducted with a young woman named Katie, from Diane's English class:

Elizabeth: So, like, sometimes, you said sometimes somebody [in your family] will read an article out loud or something. Do your parents read the newspaper...

Katie: Yeah.

Elizabeth: ...or magazines and stuff like that? So you have a lot of that kind of stuff? Do they get the *Tribune*? *The Salt Lake Tribune*?

Katie: Yeah.

Elizabeth: Do they get any magazines, or do you get any?

Katie: I get *YM*, [inaudible], you want me to name all the magazines we get? We get like [inaudible] we get *Entertainment Weekly*, and *People* magazine, and *Soap Opera Digest*.

Elizabeth: [Inaudible] I can't keep up.

Katie:	We get a lot. I can't even name 'em. My sister like orders everything.... We just get a lot of magazines, we have so many at our house.
Elizabeth:	Do you get stuff like *Time* or *Newsweek* or anything like that?
Katie:	No. (Laughs.)
Elizabeth:	What's *YM*? I know...
Katie:	*Young and Modern.*
Elizabeth:	Oh Young and...
Katie:	It's just like a teenage magazine.

We talk briefly about the body image project that I had presented in their class the prior year because I had used some of the same magazines for my research.

Katie:	Some of the articles in there are stupid though. They're like...they give you like totally wrong advice to do some things.... It's just like, I buy it for like the trauma-rama stuff.
Elizabeth:	Trauma-rama, what's that?
Katie:	It's like where they write, um, embarrassed, like where people turn in their embarrassing moments and stuff. Those are so funny.
Elizabeth:	Have you ever sent one in?
Katie:	No. (Laughs.)

Katie goes on to talk about how many of the articles focus on weight, saying, "I know, like last month's magazine is how much fat is too much, or whatever.... I mean that was stupid."

From the first part of our interview, I learned that Katie and her family read a great deal at home. Their reading consisted mainly of popular cultural texts (such as entertainment and fashion magazines), or at least this is what Katie identified with and enjoyed. At this point in her life she took a dismissive, but not necessarily critical, view of articles focusing on weight and beauty, which could mean that she would be open to discussions of such topics in classes such as physical education or biology, although it could also mean that she did not really attach much importance to such issues. Her comment about getting *Young and Modern* for the "trauma-rama" section suggested that she liked to read personal life stories about youth her age. Finding ways to connect these real-world, personal life stories to other literatures or to historical events might be a way to make content meaningful for Katie (and her classmates) in English and social studies classes. In the interview, when I pressed Katie a bit more on other reading materials, she revealed that she also liked to read popular literature:

Elizabeth: So what else do you read at home? Just you or anybody in your family.

Katie: I love to read V.C. Andrews.

Elizabeth: Oh yeah.

Katie: I'm reading her one book right now. I'm reading, I've like read the series of books. They were the first books I read.

Elizabeth: You like what series?

Katie: Um, her series…

Elizabeth: Oh, her series.

Katie: …the *Flowers in the Attic* [by V.C. Andrews], and all of those other ones. I've read all of those and I'm on the last one right now.

Elizabeth: So what, what's kind of the main theme behind 'em? Aren't they kind of scary? Aren't they like suspenseful?

Katie: Yeah…. That's why I like 'em.

Elizabeth: Mystery and…

Katie: They're kinda twisted.

Elizabeth: Yeah. That's what I thought. They're like horror though, right?

Katie: Yeah.

Elizabeth: You like that?

Katie: Yeah, they're real [inaudible].

In this segment I learned that Katie read more than popular cultural magazines; she also read fiction, and particularly horror and suspense genres such as those written by V.C. Andrews. It would make little sense to offer Katie or her peers a curriculum of books they are already reading, so I would not bring Andrews's books into the classroom. Instead, I would use the interview information to direct Katie (and her classmates) toward other suspense books. I might also ask her to bring one of her favorite books in the series to class so that we might engage in a plot and style analysis. We might discuss, as a class, why so many adolescents enjoy V.C. Andrews's work. We might then analyze other suspense books in comparison to the books in the Andrews series.

In the next segment, I asked Katie about the poetry that she began to write during her eighth-grade year, after she left the writing workshop class:

Elizabeth: Do, do you read any books that inspire your poetry?

Katie: Hmm, no. Not really, I don't know.

Elizabeth: Well where do you get ideas for all this stuff?

Katie: I don't know, just sometimes I just sit down and try, I just [inaudible] it's not like, I can't just sit down and write. It takes a long time for me. Like if I'm in the mood to write it'll take hours and hours to write and then I'll just keep it, like this little paper and I'll just rewrite it and make it the way I want it. And sometimes when I'm watchin' movies or something.

Elizabeth: You'll be writing…

Katie: Yeah….Yeah, like the one about suicide or whatever, I wrote. That one I got from a [inaudible] show, 'cause I've never committed suicide or tried, it's just that I thought about how cool, I mean, not cool, but how my personal life, how I think it should be.

Elizabeth: Which poem is it?

Katie: It doesn't even have a title, I didn't think I named it…. 'Cause I couldn't find a name. It's right here…"Screams."

Elizabeth: Oh yeah.

Katie: Yeah, it starts right there, it's a pretty long one…. And I'm all, that's, in my personal opinion, that's my favorite one.

Elizabeth: It's really good.

Katie: I think that's the one I did best at, or whatever…. So, I mean, that's my best one.

From this portion of the interview, I learned that Katie could self-analyze her writing. She could describe her motivations for writing, and she knew when something needed to be revised. She evaluated the poem as her best one, even though she also revealed in another part of the interview that the poem made her parents uncomfortable. In other words, at this point Katie was experimenting with ideas and forms for expressing those ideas that allowed her to construct an identity independent from—but not removed from—her parents. Her willingness to share the poem with her parents suggests a close relationship, but one in which Katie was trying to define herself as an equal, someone with her own thoughts, ideas, and fears. This is important information to remind us, as teachers, that adolescents are engaged in serious identity construction; they are not just a bundle of raging hormones (see Finders, 1998/1999). Katie talked more about constructing an identity and wrestling with weighty matters in the final section of the interview:

Elizabeth: And this came from a movie?

Katie: Well…

Elizabeth: I mean, the idea, like you were—

Katie: Yeah, 'cause I was watchin' a show about this kid, he commits suicide or whatever…. Sometimes, my friend likes to write too. But she like writes songs or whatever. Or like she'll take my poems and turn 'em into a song…. But I don't really like that [inaudible]. 'Cause I like, that's my poem book there, and then she did that without asking me. And then…I like my work to be my work and not hers. You know, I don't like people to change it or whatever. I like it to, I mean, if I want it to change I'll change it…. I mean, if she would have asked, I mean, 'cause there would be certain ones I wouldn't let her do it to, like, my suicide one. I wouldn't let her do that to it.

Elizabeth: Yeah, that doesn't seem like a song.

Katie: I know. See, 'cause I'd be giving people the wrong message I think. Like sometimes I'll share my work but it's for me, it's not for like everyone else, you know. (Laughs.)

Elizabeth: Right.

Katie: So…

Elizabeth: No, I think that's, I mean, a lot of times you just write to kind of get something, kind of work somethin' out in your head or whatever.

Katie: That's what I do sometimes, a lot. Like in, feelings, and all the other ones, like [inaudible] emotions and all this, that's me…. I'll just write about me.

> **Elizabeth:** So, you didn't write these poems, or even stuff like this during writer's workshop. Why?
>
> **Katie:** I don't know, I just, I didn't write, I mean, I was [inaudible] story thing or whatever. And I don't even know when I started to write. I think, my first poem was my mountain one. And like, I read that to a couple people and they liked it. And so that's, I guess, when I got my confidence. 'Cause I can't just sit down and write a poem, it takes a long time for me.... Like sometimes I'll sit down and feel like I want to write but I can't write it 'cause I got like bad writer's block or somethin'. So it just happens whenever, you know. I guess last year it didn't happen. (Laughs.)

As with the previous segment, this final portion of the interview revealed Katie as someone who was aware of her writing decisions, even if she was not completely able to control them. Because I had worked with Katie in the writer's workshop the previous year, this portion of the interview shocked me. In the writer's workshop, Katie rarely appeared serious. If I had been asked to identify students who would be likely to write at home, when on their own, I would not have chosen Katie. And yet Katie was writing at home, inspired at times by events around her or by movies she watched. She and friends obviously shared their poetry—although Katie resented her friend's appropriation of her poem—thus using poems as both communicative and identifying devices in their everyday practices.

Katie's explanation of her struggle to write in writer's workshop is also very important: It just didn't happen last year. This is a perfectly reasonable explanation, but how often are we, as teachers, willing to entertain such an explanation from our students? Anyone who writes knows that deep and meaningful writing is not something that can be forced out. And yet that is exactly what we ask students to do, whether during writer's workshop or in essay exams in science or history. Katie's comments also led me to analyze why she (and her classmates) did not bring writing from home to their writer's workshop experiences. My analyses suggest that the social, cultural, and political climate of the school—which for many students was very different from that of their homes, neighborhoods, and peer or ethnic groups—led students to keep their out-of-school literacy practices separate from the practices in which they engaged during school, even during the writer's workshop. Specifically, although the school was in a diverse urban area, that area was embedded in a community dominated by White, European American, middle-class perspectives and values. The students in Diane's classes often constructed stories that they felt would fit within the mainstream practices of the classroom, school, and community (recall Chile's writing from Chapter 3 as another example of this phenomenon). As a result, students' official workshop writings focused on events such as camping trips, visits with family, and pets. In several instances students admitted to "cleaning up" their writing for the classroom audience (for more on this analysis, see Moje, Willes, & Fassio, in press; see also, Fassio, 1999).

Reflection Point

Try using the questions in Box 4-2 to conduct an interview (or several interviews) with a student you're currently teaching. It will probably feel a bit awkward for both you and the student at first, so conducting more than one interview and asking questions in an informal setting or within regular classroom activities (during individual work time or a writing conference, for example), might be the best approach for these initial, trial interviews. I also recommend that you read Nicholson's (1984) article in which he describes "concurrent interviewing." He gives excellent advice on how to avoid putting words in students' mouths and pushing students to respond before they've had adequate time to think. He also offers a method of interviewing that focuses on what students learn in school, versus the questions in Box 4-2 that probe out-of-school stories and experiences.

Once I complete an interview, I look for information that can help me revise my teaching and choices of texts or activities, or information that can help me make suggestions for the students' work in my class. In

---

BOX 4-2
Suggested Student-Teacher Interview Questions

- What do you most enjoy doing when you're not in school?
- Do you read outside of school?
- What kinds of materials do you read?
    - Why do you read these materials?
    - Where do you get your reading materials?
    - How often do you read?
- Do you write outside of school?
    - What do you write?
    - Why do you write?
    - How often do you write?
- Who do you hang out with?
    - Do you spend time with other kids from school?
    - Do you spend time with kids in your neighborhood?
    - Do you spend time with relatives (siblings, cousins, parents)?
- Where do you hang out?
- Who is an important person in your life? Why? In what ways does that person use reading and writing?

---

addition, I find it useful to look across a number of transcripts from interviews with different students to note if there are any patterns evident in the data. One thing that I learned, for example, from interviewing Diane's students is that a significant number of them had experienced a workshop approach in previous grades. This led Diane and me to wonder whether students needed to continue the focus on expressive writing and narrative that we had emphasized in our first semester of the workshop. This pattern, combined with our own feeling that students needed to learn other kinds of writing, encouraged us to revise the workshop so that the students engaged in inquiry projects in which they examined social, community, or family issues. We also learned, from interviews with Katie, Chile, and a number of the other students, that they had read and enjoyed novels like *The Giver* (Lowry, 1993) in their elementary school years and had now developed a thirst for suspense and horror novels such as those by V.C. Andrews. This kind of information helped us in two ways: First, we knew not to ask students to read certain books because so many stu-

dents had already read them; second, although we did not want to repeat reading experiences students already had, we gained a sense of the
kinds of themes that might appeal to at least some of the students in the
class, and discovered connections that could be made from the readings
done in class (whether of literature or informational text) to the literature
and popular cultural texts youths were reading on their own (e.g., popular novels, teen magazines).

I also find that even just mentioning during class a particular experience or interest of a student that I learned from a brief conversation or a
lengthy interview can make an important connection with a student, a
connection that might make a difference in the student's learning. Last
year, for example, a university student told me after our 8-week summer
session class that I knew her better than any of her other professors at
the university. I attribute her belief to my effort to ask her routinely about
a few experiences that she had shared with me during an office visit.
Whether her assessment is accurate is less important than the fact that
she felt that we had a relationship and that the relationship made a difference when she encountered ideas in the class that she had never encountered before. Instead of dismissing the ideas or meeting them with
skepticism, she read or listened further and tried to incorporate them
into her beliefs about teaching biology. She did not simply take up the
ideas without question, but she seemed willing to explore the ideas because she felt a sense of rapport or trust. (I did find in my research with
Landy's students that several of them accepted the reading and study
strategies she suggested in large part because, as they said, they trusted
her; see Moje, 1996.)

Building a Responsive Curriculum:
An Idea for Practice

A third way that we can learn more about our adolescent students is
to build a curriculum that allows us to learn about them while they are
learning about themselves and about the world. Thus, although the following lesson is as much a way of "collecting data" about youth as it is
about teaching them, I offer it as an "idea for practice."

When Diane and I worked together in the seventh-grade writer's workshop classroom, we led the students through a biography writing project to teach the interviewing and writing skills we knew they would need for an upcoming inquiry project. Through the biography writing project, Diane and I learned a great deal about the young people in each of the classes that she taught. We found ourselves wishing that we had done the project at the beginning of the year so that we could have gotten to know the students better, and so they could have come to know one another better as well.

Begin the year by introducing a general unit concept titled something like "The Role of the Individual in Society." Such a concept could be studied in many different content areas because each discipline—from social studies to physical education, mathematics to fine art—has evolved as the result of the contributions of individuals within social systems constructed in each discipline. In an English classroom, this unit could look very much like what Diane and I did with the biography writing unit, in which we told students that our goal was to produce a biography of each student in the classroom. We then led them in a brainstorming activity in which students developed interview questions that they might ask a partner. We did this as a whole group, without assigning partners, so that the students could think broadly about what good interview questions might be. We then put students in pairs by drawing names and asked students to revise their questions to fit what they knew about their partner.

Once the questions were revised, we asked students to write their questions on index cards so that they could organize them easily both for the interview and for later writing. Diane and I wrote our own interview questions on regular-sized paper so that they would be visible to students when we modeled the process of organizing responses. We then modeled the interview process by sitting in the middle of the room with the students around us in a circle (teachers who do not have a teaching or research partner could model the process with a student partner). After we modeled asking a few questions, the students began interviewing each other. We encouraged students to record their answers directly onto the index cards, while we recorded ours on the back of our large sheets of paper.

Using our responses, Diane and I modeled the first steps of writing a biography—going through the responses, sorting them, categorizing them, and creating a framework for writing about them. We taped our different responses on the board so that students could see them, and then we asked students for suggestions about how to put the responses in order. We discussed many different possibilities for organizing ideas so that students could experiment with different writing styles. We then wrote the first two sentences of Diane's biography as a class, working from the organizational style that I chose; I was careful to explain my style choice to students, so that they had my decision process modeled for them.

Finally, students wrote biographies and read them to each other. We collected the biographies in a class book so that students could read about one another. Their writing taught us a great deal about who they were, what they cared about, and what they knew about presenting themselves and others to the world. We stopped at this point to move into the social action projects described in Chapters 7 and 8 of this book, but a unit on the individual in society—especially one designed to develop critical awareness among students—could take the students' biographies to another level.

Specifically, to develop a pedagogy that would teach students how to analyze societal structures and practices that empower some people and disenfranchise others, one would need to go beyond the stage of individual biography writing. Students could compare their biographies to published biographies, looking for ways that the students' lives—and perhaps their writing—might parallel the lives of the individuals in the published biographies. They could also present their personal biographies in small groups, analyzing their biographies for similarities and differences either in writing style or in the experiences represented in the individual's life story. As part of this assignment, encourage students to ask questions (see Box 4-3 on the next page) about how their experiences are an artifact of their position in society (e.g., as adolescents, as citizens of a particular town or country, or as members of a particular social class or racial, cultural, or gender group).

Although these different analytic activities are geared toward work in an English classroom, the same sorts of activities could be conducted in other content areas. For example, in a social studies class, students could compare their life stories to those of people in history. They could analyze the student biographers' representations of their lives and use such

> **BOX 4-3**
> **Suggested Reflection Questions About Students' Experiences**
> - Why do you think you had this experience?
> - How did the experience make you feel?
> - Who else was involved?
> - How might the experience have been different if other people had been involved (such as parents, teachers, kids of different races, poor kids, rich kids, boys, girls)?
> - Are these kinds of experiences random? Could this happen to anyone? Who might it be more likely to affect? Who would probably not be involved? Why?
> - What aspects of school/society/your community/your family allow these experiences to occur? What aspects prohibit such experiences?

an analysis to ask questions about how the historical biographies they read depend on the biographer's perspective. A biography of John F. Kennedy, for instance, would take a decidedly different perspective if written by J. Edgar Hoover than it would if written by Robert Kennedy. In the French class I studied (see Moje, Brozo, & Haas, 1994), students constructed personal portfolios—similar to autobiographies—before embarking on a project in which they would study some aspect of French culture (via reading and writing in French). These personal portfolios helped students think about their past experiences and their goals for the future, which in turn helped them generate ideas for the French projects they hoped to pursue. Similarly, in science, mathematics, physical education, or fine arts classrooms, students could examine the life stories of people who have made important breakthroughs or have accomplished great physical or artistic feats. Students then could compare their lives to the lives of these seemingly larger-than-life individuals.

In each case, students would be learning and practicing literacy and language skills associated with interviewing, biography writing, reading, and analysis, while also learning important content information that could frame their study of the discipline for the remainder of the year. In addition, they would not only learn to examine their individual experiences, but also to see their experiences in relation to others and to the larger social structures in which they live, learn, and work. As students begin to see themselves as active agents in the world, this study of how the individual is always shaped by and shaping society will begin to build a sense of purpose—a reason for learning—that so many students seem to lack in their school lives. Finally, by observing students' writing, discussions, and analyses during the interview process, you can learn a great deal about your students, both in terms of who they are as individuals and what they know about the content area being studied.

Reflection Point _____

What ideas do you have for learning more about young people's practices, beliefs, and knowledges out of school, while also teaching them content concepts and literacy processes? Take some time either to expand the ideas that I've laid out in this section or to generate a strategy or unit of your own. If you currently work with adolescents and have some extra time in your curriculum, try teaching a unit like the one outlined in this section. Keep a reflection journal for each day you teach the unit. What seemed to go well? What did not? Most important, what are you learning about your students? What are they learning about each other and about their roles in society?

In the next chapter, I offer students' insights about teachers and teaching. I also discuss young people's relationships with teachers by illustrating that all youth—whether mainstream or marginalized, successful or struggling—identify caring teachers as the ones who have made a difference in their lives. These insights are important for thinking about literacy teaching and learning because young people's engagement in school literacy practices is shaped by and reflects the relationships they have with teachers (see Dillon, 1989; Moje, 1996; Ruddell & Haggard, 1982).

Chapter 5

"So Like It Really Mattered Anyway": Kids' Insights About Teaching and Teachers

If teachers didn't hate us so much it would be better.

Jeffrey

Jeffrey, a student I would describe as marginalized in school, is not alone in his assessment. Marginalized students are considered by school personnel to be "at risk of failure," "problem" students, or "low achievers" and, as a result, often find themselves silenced or ignored in classroom interactions. Time and time again, the young people I have taught and studied, both those who are successful and those who are marginalized, have told me that their teachers' attitudes toward them and care for them made a critical difference in their success and learning in school.

Reflection Point _____

In your journal, reflect on Jeffrey's comment: How does it make you feel to know that some students feel as if teachers "hate" them? What steps can you take to ensure that your students do not feel this way? Why would making students' experiences positive be important to literacy teaching and learning? Why might it be important to your content teaching?

_____

Caring and Building Relationships

Noddings (1984) asserts that teachers need to work from an ethic of care in which they respond to students' needs. Both research interviews and anecdotal comments from a number of young people atest to the importance of enacting caring relationships in classrooms. Consider this note from Jane, written to me 12 years after I had taught her:

> You were a friend to me when I could not befriend myself. You showed me exceptional kindness when I was only a stranger. You showed me the love I had never before seen in a friend, and in so doing, the seeds were planted which sprung to life a love of self and of others that frequently and consistently catches attention....You did see something in me that no one else could, and you took your time and your effort to not let it die, and to not let me die with it. Perhaps you did not really know where I was in those days. The darkness I entered at 16 I can in hindsight see lasted for 7 years. Past the days when I saw you no more. But who can hold on for 7 years without hope? I could not have. Because you were there, because you answered yes to the question I could not even form, I stand here today a woman full of hope.

Jane's insights were important to my growth as a teacher because they forced me to think about the ways that I had cared for and built a relationship with her. I received Jane's letter at the same time that I worked with Jeffrey and his peers, all of whom were marginalized in their school settings, all of whom felt that teachers at best felt neutral toward them and at worst, as in Jeffrey's case, hated them. Jane's letter reinforced my analysis that students were deeply affected emotionally, socially, and academically by their relationships with teachers.

Jane's words were especially important because, as she indicated in her letter, I did not know at the time how much she was struggling, and I certainly did not know that what I was doing was making a difference in her life. I was a young high school teacher trying to do my best job of teaching, and I concentrated more on knowing and communicating content concepts than on anything else. I did, however, work hard on my relationships with students because I believed that strong relationships could mitigate classroom management concerns. Thus, at the same time that Jane was struggling with self-esteem and self-confidence, I was struggling with how to care for kids without being "too friendly."

As I analyzed Jane's words I became painfully aware of the fact that Jane did not once refer to the wonderful curriculum I offered or to the excellent way that I taught United States history to her. Instead, she wrote about me being an abiding presence in her life. While I am pleased that the relationship we had was important to Jane, in many ways I am dismayed that Jane did not mention the academic aspect of our relationship. I have learned through my research in other people's classrooms that effective teaching, whether of content concepts or of literacy processes and practices, engages students by connecting to them personally and by challenging them to learn content concepts and literacy skills. Such learning can serve the dual purpose of preparing students for professional lives while supporting their development as strong, confident adults who contribute to a democratic society. Perhaps Jane would never have entered the darkness she spoke of if her other teachers and I had been better able to make content concepts important, meaningful, and engaging for her. Perhaps we could have engaged Jane in lessons and projects from which she could have learned not only content concepts but also the importance of her place in the world.

The chemistry teacher I worked with, Ms. Landy, is an example of a teacher who was able to merge her caring relationships with a strong content focus. Her students, who were mostly European American, working- or middle-class students, regularly commented on her ability to build relationships with them and to engage them in the content. Lew, for example, had this to say:

> If the teacher's more positive, you're more open in the class. So you'll end up maybe sharing some experience you had with a certain part of chemistry. You'll understand it more because you're there. You won't be just like sitting there, just taking notes, and not doing…absolutely nothing. You know, you can't be monotone when you're a teacher or anything. You know, you gotta spice things up…she [Landy] uses like, student material, you know. And gets other students to relate to what they do.

Jay, another White male, noted that Landy not only cared for her students' personal, emotional development but also cared about whether they really learned chemistry.

> I think if I told her [Landy] that I definitely didn't know how to do it [homework], and I would come in during my study hall, she'd show me how to do it and let me turn it in. That's the kind of teacher Ms. Landy is.

Some teachers I know would just correct it and tell you how to do it after they've collected it and you got a zero. *So like it really mattered anyway.* [emphasis added]

Jay's comment "so like it really mattered anyway" echoes the comments of all the students I have worked with throughout my research career. Whether a struggling or successful student in school, each one commented at one time or another that they often failed to see how what they were doing in school mattered. As I will illustrate later in this chapter, many of them constructed purposes for schooling that had little to do with learning, but had everything to do with future success in college or in their chosen professions. In that way, they made school matter. What mattered to them, however, was not what they were learning, but rather what they believed they would be able to achieve in the future as a result of having good grades, certain experiences, or a diploma. On the other hand, those who were not successful in such ways found little that mattered in school.

In addition to the ability to provide students with a sense of purpose to make chemistry and literacy matter, Landy combined a sense of humor with strong content knowledge and an ability to respond to students' needs. Humor and spontaneity played an important role in the way students related to Landy and in her ability to engage them in chemistry learning:

Tyler:	She [Landy] is the best teacher in the whole school.
Noreen:	She's the best teacher, ever.
Elizabeth:	Why?
Tyler and Noreen:	We respect her.
Elizabeth:	Why?
Tyler:	She knows her material. She makes it fun. She says funny things.
Noreen:	Ms. Landy doesn't know what she's doing before she gets into class.
Tyler:	I think she does—
Noreen:	—But she goes off on tangents.
Tyler:	No, that's stupid. She knows what she's going to do, but she has a sense of humor.
Noreen:	She has a general idea, but she doesn't memorize everything.

What is ironic about Noreen's belief that Landy "went off on tangents" is that Landy was one of the most organized, planful teachers I have ever met. It was her planfulness, however, combined with her understanding of who young people are and of science content, that allowed her to be responsive to most students' needs. Landy was conscious of the need to care for kids while also engaging them in learning both content concepts and process skills, as illustrated by her response to the question, "What does it mean to you when you say you care about kids?"

> To care? To make sure that when they come into my class they feel good about themselves. To care means to do my best to make sure that they succeed at something, to make them feel that they, you know, "I can be liked by somebody." To care enough to take the time when you see a student that's having trouble to say "Hey, I have time to help you," and not turn your back the other way. And in caring I want them to learn to care about themselves…. When I care about my students, I want to see them do the best they can in my class, and prepare them to do well when they get out. I really want them to say, "Gee, you know, what I learned here has had a significant impact on my life. The way I do things."

Reflection Point

Take some time to write in your journal your thoughts about your own strengths as a teacher. Do you have strong knowledge of your content? Do you feel like you know kids and relate well to them? In what ways do you bring humor and spontaneity to your teaching? If you could change something about your teaching based on what you've read here, what would it be? How would you go about making such changes?

Why Is Caring Important to Literacy Learning in the Content Areas?

Students feeling that they are respected and cared for is important to literacy teaching for a number of reasons. First, my research indicates that when kids feel cared for—when they believe they are working in a relationship with a teacher—they tend to be more willing to try different literacy practices and strategies that the teacher offers (see Moje, 1996). Students in Landy's chemistry class, for example, indicated that they used particular literacy strategies to learn chemistry (for instance, to read their textbooks, take notes, solve problems, and engage in lab exercises) because Landy taught the strategies, not necessarily because they saw them as universally applicable strategies. One young man who resisted using the note-taking strategy Landy taught (SQ3R; see Robinson, 1946) eventually offered the strategy as evidence of Landy's effectiveness as a teacher; he explained that although he did not personally need the strategy, Landy's teaching of it was useful for many other kids in the class. He saw it as an indication of her caring and of her ability to support students' learning.

By contrast, in the French classroom of Jayne Haas, students rejected the portfolio project strategy that we developed. In many of their explanations for their resistance to the projects, students mentioned their former French teacher of 3 years and the kinds of activities, goals, and structures she had provided in the class. Our analysis indicated that the projects might have been more successful had the students been able to develop more of a relationship with Jayne, a relationship that would allow them to experiment with different ways of learning French. We had jumped into a potentially rich and fruitful pedagogy without first building relationships with the students, who needed such relationships in order to take the risks demanded by a pedagogy very different than that to which they were accustomed.

Caring relationships are also important to support the small-group work suggested by currently popular experience-based, collaborative and cooperative approaches (such as literacy workshop or project-based pedagogy). Small-group work is dependent on the development of strong teacher-student and student-student relationships in which kids engage in many kinds of Discourse. Several studies have indicated that students of all ages bring discriminatory practices to their interactions with one another and with teachers, and that many students are silenced in these group interactions (Alvermann, 1995/1996; Davies, 1989; Evans, 1996; Fassio, 1999; Lensmire, 1994; Walkerdine, 1990). If we do not develop, and thus model, caring relationships with our students, then our students will struggle to develop positive relationships with one another. The idea of caring relationships should not suggest, however, that there is no disagreement in such relationships (see Thompson, 1997). Relationships always have the potential for conflict, but conflict can be productive if students learn how to value ideas that oppose theirs and how to work through conflict in respectful and supportive ways.

Thus, critical thinking and literacy depend on both strong relationships with other people and facility with not just one kind of Discourse, but with the different Discursive practices of many communities and of the culture of power. In particular, my most recent study of social action projects in seventh-grade English classrooms indicates that if students do not have strong relationships that support open talk, alternative views, and productive conflict with their peers and teachers, then it will be difficult for students to engage in critical analysis of relationships in broader, outside-of-school settings. This was particularly important in group and whole-class work when members of the groups represented different ethnicities, peer cultures, social class positions, or genders (see Moje, 1999).

A group of students who studied gangs, for example, was composed of young women who were not gang members and those who were fringe members of gangs. Although two members had personal experience with gang practices, they drew on none of their experience, preferring to obtain all their information for the report from books and interviews with teachers and other authorities. They were unwilling to reveal the extent of their knowledge in their small group despite their belief that much of the information obtained and claims made about gangs were uninformed. Power relations within the group combined with the anti-gang climate of the school to silence the two group members who had knowledge to share. Instead of learning how to talk openly, to resist dominant constructions of people and groups as problems, and to reframe social problems in multiple ways (to generate what Aronowitz and Giroux [1991] refer to as "countertexts"), these young women learned to stay silent. Similarly, in whole-class performances we observed members of different groups keeping silent while others held the floor in discussions about social issues. My analysis led me to conclude that Diane and I had asked these youth to challenge large-scale social relations, but had not helped them think about the relationships within the classroom. As a result, their conversations about the larger social relations were at times artificial.

Silencing and Dismissal

In contrast to the students represented in Landy's class, each of whom could be considered successful in school, the kids whom I identified as marginalized spoke only in negative terms about their teachers. As illustrated in the opening comment, Jeffrey felt that teachers "hated" him. He repeated this perspective time and time again, as illustrated in this interview comment:

Jeffrey: That's why I'd always hate, like in class, something happens and they don't know who it was, they'd blame me for it. Just 'cause I had the reputation.... I always used to tell them about that, and they'd just say, "Well, what do you expect?"...Like Ms. S. always used to do that.

Later in the interview, when we discussed why we needed to use a pseudonym to refer to him, Jeffrey made this comment about respect, a theme he repeated often:

Elizabeth: The fake name is meant to keep you from being, um, so that if anybody ever read it they wouldn't say, "oh, that's [I use his real name here]," you know?

Jeffrey: "A bad kid."

Elizabeth: "A bad kid, doesn't respect his teachers or he talks back to his teachers," you know what I mean? It's just a way to keep your identity—

Jeffrey: Well, why would you respect the teacher if they don't respect you?

Elizabeth: Well, that's a really good question. I don't know.

Jeffrey: So that's like most of the teachers that I get in trouble with; they didn't respect me, so I wouldn't respect them.

It is important to acknowledge that I found Jeffrey difficult to work with in class. I taught the English class several times, and I struggled to keep Jeffrey focused, to draw on and channel his energy in positive ways, and to be patient with him. After a year of observing him, however, I noted that Jeffrey's responses and questions in the English class were often insightful and probing. His questions were not idle or only interjected to disrupt the class. Nevertheless, even in Diane's class, in which she and I worked so diligently to bring students' interests and experiences to bear on their reading and writing, many of Jeffrey's contributions were overlooked or silenced, as illustrated in this class discussion of a short story the class was reading:

Diane is talking about the temperature difference indicated in the story, 44 degrees versus 102 degrees. She asks where the students in the story went to school. One student answers, "France."

Jeffrey:	Oh, the numbers are different!
Diane:	What system do they use? (She does not acknowledge Jeffrey's response.)
Marianne:	Fahrenheit.
Kevin:	(whispered) Celsius.

I nod to Kevin and encourage him to speak up.

Kevin:	Celsius.
Diane:	Right. Now, why was he [the character in the story] crying?
Jeffrey:	Maybe he got worse.

Diane doesn't respond to Jeffrey's answer. She waits for someone else to respond.

Katie:	He was happy that he was better.

Diane goes on to talk about how people often cry out of relief, rather than out of grief. Jeffrey interrupts her:

Jeffrey:	Why do the stories in this book end at one point?
Diane:	How do you want them to end?
Jeffrey:	I don't know, they should go on.
Diane:	Then they wouldn't be short stories.

Diane resumes talking about the example she was giving.

As this example illustrates, Jeffrey was very involved in the discussion. He listened intently, offered responses—both of which were logical—and thought beyond the point of the particular story to raise questions about the genre. But Diane failed to respond. Instead of using this question as a way to engage students in thinking about the purpose and power of short story versus that of a novel, Diane continued with her point. Why? In part, because Diane had a teaching goal, a particular point that she wanted students to get from the discussion. Anyone who has taught for even a short time knows how difficult it can be to keep a discussion flowing, so Diane's reluctance to follow Jeffrey's line of thinking is to some extent understandable. But other factors also play a part in Jeffrey's silencing: First, in class he was often discourteous—at least from a mainstream perspective—in making his responses. He routinely cut others off, yelled, or changed the flow of the conversation. He also often spoke in a tone that suggested he was not serious, even when his comments were on target or insightful.

Second, Jeffrey's analysis of his teachers' treatment of him was accurate: His reputation—based on his "gangsta-style" dress and, at least in part, on his Latino ethnicity—shaped the way teachers interacted with him, even on the first day of class. As I have already discussed, teachers and students bring certain understandings, beliefs, and values to their interactions with one another. As they continue to interact on the basis of those beliefs, they continue to construct meanings about who the other person is. Jeffrey's actions in all his classes in many ways supported the beliefs that a number of his teachers already had about Latino students who dressed like "gangstas," making it difficult for his teachers to listen carefully to *what* he said, rather than to *how* he said it. Other students were able to engage in very similar interaction patterns, but they were not dismissed or overlooked in the same way. His dress, his loud interruptions, and his aggressive body language often masked an intelligent, thoughtful way of knowing the world.

In contrast to Jeffrey, students like Khek were not disruptive or openly resistant in class. Instead, they made themselves—with the help of their teachers—invisible. When discussing Khek's mathematics class with her, she told me that her teachers did not call on her to answer problems in class. In fact, she said that even when calling on students by going down every row teachers would "just like look away and say the next person's name" when they got to Khek. Sadly, this was not a one-time occurrence, nor was it something Khek disliked. In discussing her English class, Khek said:

Khek: She's [the English teacher] nice. She gives me good grades
           and all this stuff. Even though, I mean, I think I deserve
           the grade she gives me, and I think she's way nice. She
           don't pick on me, and I just love that, like to read stuff,
           she don't pick on me. I don't know why, I just love it
           though.

Elizabeth: Do you think that she's "nice" to other people, too?

Khek: The only person I see this happening is to me.

Elizabeth: You mean you're the only person she's never picked on
           to read?

Khek: So far as I know.

Elizabeth: Oh.

Khek: Well, I mean, she did it once but she hasn't been doin' it
           for a while.

Elizabeth: I wonder how you luck out. It seems kind of funny.

Khek: I like it, though. I think she knows that because there are
           times that she'd be like, she looks over by me, and I'm
           writing or something, I always do that.

Khek believed that this practice of not engaging students who either
struggled with reading or who did not appear to enjoy oral reading (as
was the case with Khek, who could read proficiently, if not with expression or enthusiasm) was directed only at her, but my observations indicate
otherwise. I found, in fact, in each of my classroom-based studies that as
long as students were not disruptive, teachers often did not include those
who appeared uncomfortable with or distanced from whole-group reading or discussion. This practice, unfortunately, was most often applied to
young women, and particularly to young women of color. Unfortunately
both successful and struggling students experienced (and enjoyed) this
invisibility. Heather, from Landy's class, for example, preferred to take
notes rather than to discuss, solve problems, or even engage in laborato-
ry exercises (see Dillon & Moje, 1998). Another young woman in Landy's
class spoke of the teacher's failure to require the student to "go to the
board" (a routine class activity) as the teacher's way of taking care of the
student in the class because she was very shy. In the two English classes
that I studied, at least one young woman did not speak aloud in any
whole-group activity during the entire first semester of the class (she

transferred out at the end of that semester), and several others rarely spoke—usually speaking only when Diane asked them direct questions— during class discussions.

This practice on the part of teachers is rarely malicious and is constructed in interaction with students, as Khek's "I just love it, though," comment illustrates. The good intentions behind this practice, together with the realization that students help to support such practice, underscore the importance of teachers' self-reflections. At times, we overlook students unconsciously, simply because they are quiet. At other times, we enact a form of classroom management either by engaging those who are disruptive (and thus overlooking those who are quiet) or by ignoring those who disrupt routinely. On one occasion, for example, when I taught in Diane's English class, I found myself interacting with only one side of the room while two rows of the class—virtually all young women, together with two young men of color—said nothing. Even after I realized what we (the students and I) were doing, I struggled to involve them because I had so many students on the other side of the room vying to speak in the discussion. It is true that the quiet students may have preferred to remain quiet; kids have different learning preferences, and we should honor those preferences to some extent. However, this invisibility or dismissal of students who are either quiet or struggling has enormous consequences for both social and academic learning. Consider for example, what Anthony and Alex have to say about their science class:

Alex: I didn't have to do anything in science and still pass.

Anthony: I didn't even do that.

Elizabeth: You didn't even do it?

Anthony: No.

Alex: I didn't do it, not even my test.

Elizabeth: And you passed?

Alex: Yeah. And I was absent in that class 72 times. My teacher just liked me.

Elizabeth: Wow. You think that's good?

Anthony: Yeah.

Alex: Yeah.

Anthony and Alex's comments reflect more than the bragging about lack of effort that we sometimes hear adolescents engage in when they talk about school. My observations of and interactions with Anthony over the course of 2 years suggest that he engaged in a bare minimum of work in school and that he was rarely excited about or engaged in the activities offered. These insights are especially important because in more than one interview Anthony expressed an interest in becoming a doctor, and he was involved in a special science and mathematics program for students who appeared to have an aptitude for those disciplines. Simply passing in science without doing any work did not serve either young man very well.

Reflection Point

Describe in your journal a typical day in your classroom. Do any of your practices serve to silence or dismiss your students? How? Who gets silenced? Who gets dismissed? Then, over the next week, keep track of who speaks in your classroom. (If you can't find someone to observe you, then I recommend videotaping.) Note the color, gender, and behavioral patterns of the kids who do and do not speak. Note whether you call on them or they volunteer. Compare this to what you wrote before making explicit observations, then analyze the data you collected: Are there any patterns in kids' participation? What might you do to bring them into the conversation? To engage them?

Why Does Silencing Matter to Literacy Learning in the Content Areas?

The silencing, dismissal, or rendering invisible of certain students is problematic in part because it indicates that caring relationships are not being developed, or that teachers and students are enacting relationships of care in ways that have negative consequences for the students (for example, assuming that it is better to allow a student to become invisible rather than to "put her on the spot"). If caring relationships are a critical aspect of student success, as the students in my study seemed to believe, and if caring relationships make a difference in how kids take up particular literacy practices that their teachers offer, then the youth who are being silenced or dismissed are at a disadvantage because either they are not part of a caring relationship, or they are engaged in misguided relationships that allow them to disappear rather than learn to claim a voice for themselves.

The silencing is also troubling because it means that students are not talking, reading, and writing in ways that support their literacy development. If literacy learning in secondary content classrooms involves learning how to engage in and navigate different Discourse communities (such as the science community or the community of sport and recreation), then students need to be engaged in and practicing the Discourses of those communities. A great deal of research on classroom interaction already suggests that adolescent students in general do not have opportunity to do much talking, especially in secondary school classrooms (see Alvermann, Dillon, & O'Brien, 1987; Goodlad, 1984; Sizer, 1984). The kids' insights represented in this chapter expand on this research by suggesting that some students—in particular poor, young women of color—are actually made invisible, dismissed from the little talking, reading, and writing that does occur in their classrooms.

If adolescents are not talking, reading, and writing in their content classes then they probably are not learning the literacy and language skills necessary for critical thinking and critical literacy development. Opportunities to engage in oral language enhance writing and reading skills (Alvermann, Dillon, & O'Brien, 1987; Barton, 1995) and young people need opportunities to talk about their ideas—whether ideas for creative writing or ideas for a research project—in order to refine, clarify, and extend thinking. Practicing both discourse and Discourses, to use Gee's (1996) distinction, is especially important in classrooms wherein students are learning not only a new Discourse, but also a new language. For example, consider this exchange between a teacher and a student in a seventh-grade, bilingual immersion science classroom, in which my colleagues and I had been studying the enactment of project-based science (for more on this, see Moje, Collazo, Carrillo, & Marx, 2000):

> Maestro Tomas [the teacher] begins the discussion in Spanish with the unit's driving question [the question that frames the project inquiry the class will be doing], "*Cuál es la calidad del rio?*" [What is the quality of water in the river?] He then explains in Spanish that they will be studying the river in order to learn about water quality. He then repeats the driving question in English. As he does this one of the students asks, "Maestro, what is quality?"
>
> Maestro Tomas responds, "I am glad that you asked that because I want you to rate what you think water quality is on a scale from 0-5." He continues in Spanish: "*Vamos a discutir la calidad del rio*" (We are going to discuss the quality of the river). As he writes on the board [in English], he explains the rating scale in Spanish.

This excerpt from field notes illustrates the importance of engaging students in discussion that draws from both the technical vocabulary and the themes that underpin different disciplines. The student who asked "What is quality?" struggled not only with the English (the maestro's initial question was in Spanish) but with what the word *quality* meant in relation to science and tests of the river. As Cummins (1984) and Wong-Fillmore (1982) have argued, there are significant differences between learning the social and academic Discourses of a second language. Students need opportunities not only to hear teachers saying technical words and enacting Discourses of the different disciplines, but also to try these words out in conversations and written works. Silent students, therefore, are students who are not engaging in the many Discourses critical to learning in the content areas.

The previous excerpt also points toward the possibility of working through problems together so that students can hear the teacher's and fellow students' thoughts and speech. The following comment from Craig, a young man in Landy's classroom, illustrates how students can learn from one another's discourse:

Craig: I like, I like the idea of kids going up to the front [to work problems on the board for the class] because a lot of times, you know, you can learn by their mistakes. And also sometimes another kid can explain it to you once he understands it maybe better than a teacher can, just because they think on different terms.

Elizabeth: Do you think that having to explain it, the actual act of having to talk about it and say what this means, makes a difference?

Craig: Yeah. I didn't think it did, but the other day when I explained mole [a term that denotes an amount of matter equal to 6.02×10^{23} particles of matter] to Noreen.... I didn't understand it until I explained it to her. 'Cause I was lost on it, too. And then I started thinking, and then I said, well wait a second, that's how it is. And once I said it to her, then I understood it, too.

A bit later in the interview the discussion continues:

Elizabeth: So, do you like that you get to hear people's ideas because that lets you know that everybody thinks differently?

Craig: Yeah. And, you know, just a lot of times there's a lot of different ways you can look. There's a lot of different ways you can look at a mole and still understand it. And a lot of times if somebody else shows their view on it, you can keep yours, and also think about theirs, and have a wider understanding.

Missing Purpose

Sure I might learn more from this approach [portfolios], but that's not really what high school is all about. It's just about getting into college.

Mike, 1989

Mike, a 12th-grade honors student, used these words to explain his resistance to the project-based pedagogy that we offered in his fourth-year French class. While Mike's words can be attributed to the condition commonly referred to as "senioritis" by veteran high school teachers and students, his words reflect an attitude that prevails among all levels of secondary school students, whether they are succeeding or struggling in school. For example, every one of the struggling seventh graders I interviewed commented that their junior high school grades "didn't matter" because their grade point averages would not be figured until ninth grade. Many of them commented that they would start working hard then, when it "counted." This exchange took place between Anthony, Anthony's friend Alex, and me:

Elizabeth: Okay, tell me this, so you guys both think you want to be doctors or lawyers, or you definitely want to go to college, right?

Alex: Yeah.

Elizabeth: So how are you going to do that? Let's say you go to school all the time but your teachers don't give you much homework and you don't read and you don't write and you don't do any projects. How are you gonna learn enough to go to college?

Anthony: Uh...

Elizabeth: I mean, where do you think you should learn that? And I'm real serious about this.

Anthony: High school.

Elizabeth: Oh. So it's all gonna change, now you're gonna want to read...

Alex : Yeah.

Anthony: Yeah.

Elizabeth: ...and you're going to want to write and you're going to do all your homework.

Alex : 'Cause it's actually gonna count now.

Elizabeth: Oh. So you think junior high's just kind of a waste?

Alex : Yeah.

Anthony: Yep.

Alex : It don't count, it's not on your records. Ninth grade is, so you gotta try.

Elizabeth: Hmm. Do you think that what you did in seventh and eighth grade, that counselors will look at that at all and that might influence the opportunities you get in ninth grade?

Anthony: I didn't do nothin' in seventh and eighth grade.

Elizabeth: Well that's what I mean. I mean, what if I were your ninth-grade teacher and I got your records from seventh and eighth grade. I mean, you say they don't count, right? But somebody marks down what you did.

Anthony: They just look at it to put you, [to say] what class [you'll take]. (Laughs.)

Alex : Then you can, like, take a test and they might put you up [into a more advanced class].

Elizabeth: They might?

Anthony: They could.

Elizabeth: But if you didn't do any work in seventh and eighth grade, you didn't learn anything, then how will you do well on the test?

Anthony: Um, cheat.

Alex: You might actually know of it.

Elizabeth: I gotta tell you, I don't want you to be my doctor, not if you're going to cheat your way through school.

In addition to the fact that these boys' belief that "grades don't count" is misguided because grades *are* used to determine which classes students will be allowed to take once they enter high school, these comments also indicate the belief that school is not about learning for these students. The fact that they were only going to "work hard" when grades counted, suggests that they saw getting grades as the purpose of school.

In another interview with Jay, the 10th-grade student from Landy's chemistry class quoted previously, Jay discussed his reliance on cheating as a means of survival in high school. His words illustrate a perspective similar to Mike's, that the value of schooling is measured only in terms of getting the grades necessary for entrance to college:

Elizabeth: Would you cheat in Ms. Landy's class if you didn't think you'd get caught?

Jay: Oh, for sure. I don't mean to.... I mean, if you would have an "A" or a "C," who wouldn't want the "A"?

Elizabeth: So, you'd cheat and not study and not learn anything? Or...?

Jay: Yep.

Elizabeth: Just so you'd get the "A"?

Jay: 'Cause I've seen, like, my friend Jim, he has two brothers who are in college, and they got like "Ds" all the way through high school. But then when they went to college they were on the Dean's List. So...but, when I get in college, though, I'll...

Elizabeth: Then you won't cheat anymore?

Jay: Well, I mean I'll cheat...I don't know.

Elizabeth: Aren't you afraid that if you cheat and you don't learn anything, you won't do well in college?

Jay: Well, every class...(he pauses, then shrugs)...I'm not worried about it.

At a later point in the interview, another student joined us and added this perspective on the purpose of high school:

Matt: You know somebody told me, and I'm being serious, that in high school, all you have to do is basically survive. You ask him what he thinks about cheating. Well that's just, if you don't know something, there's no other way. I guess, it's just like in life.

Jay: The man here's an example. The boy hasn't opened a book in three years of high school, and he gets "Cs."

Matt: I have the brain, you know, my parents tell me I have the brain, I know I have the brain, it's just laziness. You know, but, I mean, in some ways you just have to survive. Just like in life, if you cheat, you get ahead. It's true. Isn't it true? (I don't respond.) I mean, you're an adult, you know, so....You know, hopefully in college, in college I know you can't cheat, 'cause if you get busted, you're out, forever. You know, so in high school, I feel you gotta do what you gotta do to survive.... But I don't think it ever catches up to you because if somebody cheats, well, they're only hurting themselves, because when the final comes they're not going to do that well. But usually the finals cover the stuff that you've most recently done, and so you've gotta start kickin' it in gear towards the end of the semester.

Jay: Or you can cheat on the final.

Although they are not as explicit as Mike, both Jay and Matt implicitly express the belief that the purpose of high school is not learning. All three young men articulate a perspective that high school—and perhaps school in general—is simply something to survive. The higher the grades, the more successful one will be, not because high grades indicate learning, but because high grades ensure better chances beyond secondary school. In fact, Jay's skepticism regarding whether his lack of learning in high school will have any bearing on his success in college suggests that he sees virtually no value in the lessons of high school. Matt's comments about cheating in life beyond high school suggest that the problem stems from large social structures as well as from the learning activities that teachers offer to students in high school.

Such comments do not, of course, reflect the perspective of all kids, but they do reflect the perspective of many adolescents in our schools. (Keep in mind that Mike, Jay, and Matt were all relatively successful, well-liked, mainstream students. Jay's teachers, for example, would not have identified him as a potential cheater.) For those who are successful in school, the purpose of schooling is viewed as getting good grades in preparation for college admission or of getting the information needed to do well on college entrance exams. For those who are not successful, the purpose of schooling is seen either as a way of obtaining a diploma needed to get a basic job in society or as an activity designed to keep them off the streets. Sadly, very few students I interviewed—whether as individuals or in groups—could speak about what they learn in school. Even when I probed them by asking them to reflect on specific assignments, to read sections of text and talk with me about what sense they are making, to talk through writing they have done or notes they have taken, or to give specific applications of concepts to their lives, all students I interviewed struggled to articulate something meaningful that they had learned in school.

Reflection Point_____

In your journal write about *your perception* of the purpose for schooling. Why do students need to learn the content or skills that you teach? What do you think your students would say in response to this question? What beliefs, past experiences, or future goals are reflected in their sense of the purpose of school and education?

Why do students have such beliefs about the purpose of schooling? In part, youth are socialized in everyday interactions to see primary, and especially secondary, education in material terms, such as acquiring grades, diplomas, and future employment. The emphasis on grading and testing that pervades our school systems reinforces the importance of schooling for grades or test scores, rather than for learning. My research, however, indicates that the curricula and activities offered in school are also complicit in these beliefs about the purpose of schooling. Time and time again, the youth with whom I work tell me that their schoolwork is boring, that it does not relate to their lives, or that it lacks purpose. Some of this is due to their own struggles to define their interests and identities, but much of their missing sense of purpose in school is due to curricula and activities that do not challenge them. Chile, for example, described her eighth-grade English class in this way:

Chile:	We just got done reading *That Was Then, This Is Now* [by S.E. Hinton].
Elizabeth:	Oh yeah, that's a good book.
Chile:	And I got, I just got done reading that and…I like it but it's—she don't let us do nothin' except just sit there and read. She's like, "Just read for 25 minutes."
Elizabeth:	Do you ever sit and discuss, like…
Chile:	Huh-uh. (She shakes her head "no".)
Elizabeth:	So…
Chile:	She's like…
Elizabeth:	Kids don't get to share what they've read?
Chile:	…As soon as we're done reading, we don't even get to take turns reading, like if we're reading a book, she has it recorded. And she has us listen to the recording. And then she has a study guide, you know, like um, when um, his friend Charlie got shot, and they got, they were playin' pool or whatever, and that dude got shot?
Elizabeth:	Right.
Chile:	They're like, "what happened to Charlie," she's like, "okay, let's go over the question, what happened to Charlie, he got shot, what did na na na."
Elizabeth:	That's how she does it?
Chile:	"Na na na na na…"
Elizabeth:	And she reads the answers?
Chile:	Yeah, and then she says the answers. "Okay, now copy

> 'em down and if you don't got 'em done then copy 'em
> from the person next to you. Okay, next thing, we're
> gonna...."And I'm like, you're just like, okay (she gives a
> resigned shrug of her shoulders).

Elizabeth: So, so you, what would you say you're learning about
English, or about literacy in that class?

Chile: I don't know, I don't, nothing really. I don't, all I do, I don't
know, we don't really do nothin' except just sit there and
read....

Chile's rendition of her English class stood in stark contrast to that of
her English class from the year before, in which Chile had been asked to
write stories from her experience; to read, discuss, and write about novels;
and to engage in a group project in which students studied a social problem and presented their findings to the class. And yet, even in the writer's
workshop classroom the previous year, Chile had lost interest as the year
progressed. She had not always written from her experience. Nevertheless, I asked her to compare her experience in the writer's workshop class
with the one described in the previous dialogue:

Elizabeth: What if she had you do some writing stuff like we did
last year, would you like that?

Chile: Yeah.

Elizabeth: Yeah. But she doesn't do anything like that?

Chile: Nuh-uh. [No.]

Elizabeth: 'Cause you're such a good writer I'd like to see you write
more. I mean, it'll be good that you're, that we're gonna
write this book chapter together and maybe an article in
addition to that. It's weird, I mean, it's English class—
you'd think you'd do more.

Chile: Yeah, 'cause I liked English, I liked writing all the time.
'Cause I always got good grades for writing, always. In
elementary school I always had good grades. 'Cause I always had a lot of stories that I liked and stuff.

Note how Chile explained her preference for the writing-based class
in two terms: her interests ("I like writing") and her grades ("I always
had good grades"). Throughout our 3 years of working together, I asked
Chile several times about what she was learning in school and what pur-

pose it might serve later in life. She always evaluated her learning in terms of the grades she was getting, and not once did she connect her school learning to future goals. Given the nature of many of her classes (she described a number of classes throughout our 3 years together in similar terms, and her descriptions were validated independently in interviews with other students and teachers), it is not surprising that she had not developed a strong sense of how these experiences might serve her in the future.

It is ironic that, in contrast to students such as Chile, many successful students have come to appreciate rote, or highly structured, activities in their classes. Because they are focused on getting good grades, they find these classes useful, if not compelling. For example, Keith, another student in the French class, explained his resistance to the portfolio project, which did not emphasize rote learning and which did not offer extensive structure, with this comment about why he had taken the fourth year of French:

> I just wanted to have a break in my schedule. You know, a class where I didn't have to kill myself. This portfolio thing means that I have to do a lot of extra work. I really have to think about the stuff.

Whereas struggling students find rote, highly structured exercises stifling, those students who view the purpose of secondary school simply as a way of getting grades necessary for college admission *and* who are good at getting high grades find such exercises useful.

I observed an exception to this perspective in Landy's class, in which students valued the work and the thinking that Landy pushed them to do. My analysis of Landy's interactions with her students suggests that their willingness to work hard in her class was due in part to the relationships—ones filled with care and humor—she built with her students. However, Landy also emphasized organization and precision in her classroom. The assignments that she gave, while numerous and rigorous, were also highly structured. Although the assignments were time consuming, they had, for the most part, "right answers." As Heather stated, "Chemistry's easy for me. It's all perfect. It all works out." Thus, students were not pushed to set their own purpose or goals, nor were they given opportunities to design and carry out inquiry, except in the honors chemistry class that Landy also taught. They learned a great deal of information through their homework assignments, but end-of-the-year interviews indicate that they did not necessarily have a strong sense of the larger purpose behind learning these pieces of information. Nevertheless, students considered Landy a masterful teacher because they had learned so much information in such a rigorous, but supportive, environment. Years after she had graduated from high school, one former student of Landy's told me that she "remembered everything Ms. Landy taught." Such trust and respect is a testament to the power of Landy's caring and commitment to students. This trust and respect also indicates that students equate knowing information with learning.

Reflection Point

Over the course of the semester, try to find out what your students think about the questions I posed in the previous Reflection Point. Try to interview 5 to 10 students (choosing students of different backgrounds, ages, achievement levels, and cultures). Keep the interviews simple by asking them the same questions that you've reflected on here. You might want, however, to give them some specific concepts or skills to think about in order to make the question more concrete. For example, you might ask history students to talk about the purpose of learning about history, and then move to concepts like "democracy," "the industrial revolution," or "civil war." To analyze your findings, look for patterns in students' responses, such as "reflects teacher's perspective," "focuses on testing," "can't provide a purpose." Once you've made some general analyses, write about how you might address these beliefs.

Chapter 6

Making It Matter: On Respect, Manner, and Texts in Content Literacy Teaching

The voices of young people in Chapters 3 through 5 have highlighted a number of important points that we need to consider in our teaching. First, young people know and can do a lot before they come to our classrooms. They construct this knowledge from cultural and family funds of knowledge and from popular cultural texts such as movies, books, music, the Internet, and video games. This knowledge can serve as a rich resource for inquiry around the many content concepts suggested by state and national standards.

Second, adolescents use multiple forms of representation (e.g., Mark's African drumming; Jane's dramatic performances and paintings; Chile's films, music, and journal writing; Katie's poetry; Anthony's graffiti) in their everyday practice, but we do not use such forms very often in school. As a result, we do not teach them how to move back and forth with ease between these forms or, more important, how to know *when* to move back and forth. In other words, young people may know a great deal, and they may use many different forms to make meaning, but they are not learning to navigate different Discourse communities consciously; that is, they do not have meta-knowledge of Discourses (see New London Group, 1996). In fact, young people very rarely recognize explicitly the difference between different Discourse communities, and in some cases adolescents use literacy strategies in certain contexts simply because they connect a particular strategy with a particular teacher (see Moje, 1996).

Third, young people want to be cared for by their teachers. They want to have relationships based on mutual respect and trust. They do not want to make all decisions in their learning careers, but they do want their voices to be heard and heeded. The pattern I have analyzed in my research studies over several years is striking: Youth who feel they have been cared for by teachers tend to be successful, even when they do not see school as a learning site; youth who feel hated by or dismissed by teachers are not usually successful in school, and many of them fail to find success beyond school as well. These are important patterns, but we do not know whether success is a result of caring relationships or a precursor of them. However, if success is a result of caring, then we have to work on how we enact such relationships with young people. If success is a precursor, then we must question the impact of our expectations and assumptions about adolescents, especially those adolescents whose backgrounds differ from our own. My research suggests that student success and teacher caring represent an interactive rather than causal relationship (see also Dillon, 1989; Ladson-Billings, 1994). Teachers are likely to find it easier to care about and for youth who are successful, and young people indicate that caring teachers help them succeed. Thus, we must pursue research on the impact of caring, because teachers and researchers can make literacy and content matter in students' lives by thinking carefully about how to develop caring relationships with students.

It is also interesting to note two other patterns. First, students who are especially successful note that their teachers' care extends beyond niceness: They highlight caring teachers' abilities to make content meaningful and relevant to their lives, as well as the teachers' commitment to their learning. As Jay indicated (see Chapter 5), caring teachers communicate that the homework and class assignments that students do impact their learning, and do not simply serve as a way of assessing and assigning grades. Second, many young people do not see learning as the purpose of schooling. This is true whether students are successful or unsuccessful in school. As Mike's words from Chapter 5 indicate, successful students see schooling as a place to obtain the grades necessary to go on to college. Heather's apathy in the chemistry class— even while pondering chemistry-related questions—illustrates that Heather saw the class as a series of tasks to complete. For unsuccessful students who rarely think in terms of going on to college, the purpose of school is to achieve a diploma, at best, and to avoid detention, at worst. This is not to say that both sets of students do not *want* to learn, but rather that they do not see school as the place where real learning occurs.

Caring for young people, bringing them all into the classroom conversation so they are not silenced or dismissed, and helping them find a purpose for school-based learning are not easy tasks. Finding out more about who adolescents are, both in and out of school, is an important first step in this process. Knowing more about what young people know and care about will allow teachers not only to develop more personalized relationships, but also to make connections from content concepts to students' lives. Finding out these things, however, is challenging for both teachers and researchers if we do not first engender young people's trust and respect. It seems important that we think about what qualities show young people that teachers respect them.

Respecting Kids

Engaging in Respectful Discourse

Respect (and lack of respect) can be communicated to adolescent students in many ways, but language and other discourse practices are some of the most influential ways of communicating how teachers view students. Ms. Landy is a good example of someone who treated her students respectfully through discourse. In the 2½ years that I worked with her, she always called students by name, she never raised her voice, and she frequently asked them about their learning and their experiences out of school. Moreover, she worked diligently to make her students feel as though they were part of a community of learners and, specifically, of a community of science learners. As I illustrate in an analysis of Landy's discursive practices (Moje, 1995), she frequently used inclusive language such as, "As scientists, we say…." On one occasion she explicitly told a student to consider herself a scientist, as illustrated in this excerpt from my field notes:

Ms. L. asked Kari what "actual yield"meant. Kari hesitated, then offered,"Isn't it like what the chemists get?"Ms. L. responded by saying,"Yes.
It's what *you* get.You're a chemist, too.You'll get an actual yield in the lab."

Contrast Landy's inclusive, content-focused discourse with the words of a
teacher I observed when visiting one of Katie's classes:

As I approached Katie's art class, I heard what sounded like a
teacher's voice, yelling. I hesitated outside the door, waiting for a moment in which I could knock. None came. Standing outside the door, I became more and more dismayed at what I heard:
"And you lazy kids better get up here and pick up these stinkin' projects. I'm tired of having 'em sittin' around here!"yelled Katie's teacher.
At this point I entered the room, deciding that no break in the dia-
tribe was imminent. I looked around at a class filled with kids slouched
in their chairs at art tables. Those who were still sitting up wore expressions that communicated boredom, disgust, or distress. The others rested
their heads on arms folded on the tables, eyes closed. They didn't seem to
be learning a great deal about art.

Similarly, Jeffrey's teacher—the one he had so little respect for—communicated her lack of respect for students by speaking to them in bored
tones or by yelling at them frequently. To Jeffrey in particular, she communicated a lack of respect or care by allowing him to leave the room to
go to his locker and then locking the door so he could not re-enter class.
In this case, Jeffrey was not only silenced in the classroom, he was literally dismissed from the classroom. Although Jeffrey was admittedly a
tough kid, he was willing to give respect if given it in return. For example,
Jeffrey had immense respect for his mother, stating that "I know I may
not have respect for certain people, but I always have respect for my
mom." When I asked why, he replied,

Well, like, my mom, she works all the time, and we don't have a lot
of money, but me and my brother, we don't ask for much 'cause we know
my mom doesn't have a lot of money. My mom has to work all the time,
but she's always there for us.

Unlike the teacher who locked Jeffrey out of his classroom, Jeffrey's
mother was an abiding presence in his life. She sacrificed for him and he
was willing, in turn, to sacrifice (at least in some ways) for her.

Another way that teachers show respect for students is through their dress and appearance. It may sound trivial, but I know from both my research and my own high school and university teaching that something as simple as the way one dresses when teaching can communicate a great deal to students. Landy, for example, always dressed in what she considered a professional manner, and she did so consciously. When I asked her what it meant to be a teacher she replied,

> What it means to be a teacher. What it means to me is to be role model. A person that sets an example. Not only just expounds what they believe is true, but really lives, lives what he or she believes so that students can learn from that. And that's in the way they speak, the way they dress, the way they relate to each other. Those nonverbal kinds of communications that go on, that say a lot more sometimes than what verbally comes through.

Landy lived this philosophy: In the 2 years I worked with her, she was always dressed in formal attire. She usually wore a skirt, blouse, and low-heeled pumps; I saw her wear pants only once. On lab days she donned a white lab jacket and safety goggles. Her dress told students that she saw teaching as an important, professional task; that she saw herself as a scientist, especially during lab activities; and that she took her own safety rules seriously. She did not ask students to follow rules that she herself did not follow. Similarly, an African American teacher with whom Ladson-Billings (1994) worked dressed like a corporate executive, asserting that the way a teacher dresses means something to kids: "They [young white teachers in her district] come in here dressed like people going to scrub somebody's kitchen. I mean what kind of message do you send the children when you don't care enough to put on clean, pressed clothes?" (p. 35).

In contrast to these teachers' perspectives, a number of teachers with whom I have worked believe that *dressing down,* that is, dressing in clothes that are considered fashionable by youth, might appeal to young people and encourage them to trust teachers and to become engaged in what the teacher cares about. Both views have merit; what is most important is that these teachers are thinking about their appearance and the message they communicate to youth not only through dress but also via their gestures, body language, and facial expressions. Whether intentional or not, dress and appearance can communicate to students what teachers think of their work and of their students. It is no coincidence that media representations of teachers show the ineffective, unpleasant teachers dressed in outdated or sloppy garb, while respected teachers dress in fashionable or trademark garb.

Trusting Our Students

As teachers, we can also communicate our respect for students by believing them and accepting what they say and working with it, even when we are skeptical of its veracity. Like Luis, a young man represented in Hynds (1997), each of the struggling students with whom I worked related experiences (usually more than one) of being accused—often without evidence—of committing some classroom crime. As Jeffrey indicated (see Chapter 5), his reputation, his dress, and perhaps his color and ethnicity marked him as a problem and a suspect. Other students, however, imply that particular teachers refuse to trust *all* students:

> **Elizabeth:** What would you do to make school better?
> **Alex:** Get nice teachers.
> **Elizabeth:** Okay, let's see…
> **Alex:** Teachers that don't accuse everyone of stealing.
> **Elizabeth:** Nice teachers who don't accuse everyone of stealing?
> **Alex:** Yeah, my math teacher accuses everyone in the class of stealing.

In a related vein, students are sometimes questioned about whether the work they do is really theirs or whether they are capable of doing the work. Chile, for example, described an interaction with one of her teachers:

> For my free reading book I'm reading *The Rainmaker* by John Grisham, and my teacher, here I bring it in and she looks at me like with this look of surprise. And then I, I go, "Well, what do you think, that I am so stupid that I wouldn't have a book or couldn't have a book?" And then she's like, "I didn't say that," and I go, "What, were you surprised that I picked one that didn't, wasn't just pictures?" And she's like, "I never said that. Why don't you just sit down and take your seat?"

In a somewhat different example, Anthony brought a poem titled "Gangsta Prayer" to the writer's workshop and claimed to have written it with his friends during his lunch break. He expressed an interest to me in revising during the writer's workshop time, but Diane was not sure that he had actually written it, so she did not feel comfortable pursuing it as "his" writing. Although I could understand her perspective, I struggled with the feeling that we were losing an opportunity for teaching writing *and* that we communicated to the student that we didn't trust him. Some would argue that to accept what adolescents say at face value communicates to them that we are naive and that they can take advantage of our naiveté, especially because we know that some students do cheat or plagiarize, as illustrated by Jay's discussion of cheating. But young people deserve our respect and trust until they demonstrate otherwise—and even then, they deserve respect and care. We can make decisions about when to be "naive" and accept what a student tells us and when to challenge what students say based on what we believe the outcomes will be. In the case of "Gangsta Prayer," we could have taught Anthony writing skills as we worked on a piece that he cared about, regardless of whether he was the original author, without teaching him that plagiarism was acceptable. Doing so would have communicated an interest in his world and trust in his word.

Acknowledging Our Students' Out-of-School Lives

Another way that we can communicate our respect for students is to remember that they have lives outside of school, lives that often demand a great deal of them. In *Schoolgirls*, Orenstein (1994) writes about a young woman who was routinely truant. In one conversation with the young woman, Orenstein learned that the girl often stayed home to care for her younger sibling because her mother had to work late. The young woman was regularly given detentions and labeled as irresponsible and undeserving of education as a result of her truancy, but she actually exhibited a great deal of responsibility by not allowing her sibling to go unsupervised. Labeling and disciplining her without trying to learn about the demands in her life were disrespectful acts.

Similarly, many of the struggling youth with whom I worked had good reasons for their actions, but few people sought to find out what those reasons were. For example, Khek once missed school for 5 days because she was given an out-of-school suspension for speaking disrespectfully to a teacher. According to school policy, the suspension could not be lifted unless Khek's parents came to school to discuss the problem. Khek's parents, however, not only spoke little English but also each worked two jobs. Just getting to school to resolve the issue would be difficult and once there, Khek's parents would have found themselves at a disadvantage when conferring with school personnel. Khek eventually just returned to school, but avoided administrators so they would not realize that she was back. (When asked about the incident, a school administrator said that they had called the home several times and that Khek was not actually told to stay out of school, but rather was given an in-school suspension. Khek, however, was convinced that she had been suspended from school.) It seems ironic that Khek's offense—using disrespectful language—was met with sanctions that were, in many ways, disrespectful of her life outside of school.

By contrast, in the middle-class, predominantly White, private schools where I started my teaching career, administrators discouraged teachers from assigning homework on weekday "game nights" (most often occurring during basketball and baseball/softball seasons) or on the nights of special musical or performance events because it was recognized that these events were all-consuming in the lives of youth. Why is it that these activities were privileged, while activities such as caring for family members or working to contribute to family income are not? Why are the out-of-school obligations of some youth respected, but the obligations of others devalued? In many cases, our lack of respect stems from a lack of awareness of what young people have to do out of school. Using some of the methods discussed in Chapter 3 and 4 can help expand an understanding of and respect for what youth do out of school.

In other cases, however, lack of respect has to do with assumptions made and values held about our own and another's class, culture, gender, age, or race. This means that simply knowing about what young people do may not help to develop respect for them, because people bring assumptions and values to their understanding of others' practices. Linda McNeil (1988), for example, has illustrated that teachers in working-class schools believe their students need to be controlled more than middle or upper-class students do. According to McNeil, teachers she interviewed expressed the belief that the working class and poor people they taught not only would not go on to college but also did not have the attention span and intellectual capability to engage in sophisticated cognitive activities. Jean Anyon (1981) also writes about this phenomenon and illustrates how the texts and other print materials used in different classrooms reflect these assumptions about social class and intellectual ability. In a recent *Ann Arbor News* article, African American parents detailed assumptions made about their children, such as one upper-middle class youth being given a free-lunch card, on the basis, apparently, of the color of his skin (Tilove, 1999).

In my own research, I have watched teachers make assumptions and engage in differential treatment time and time again. These assumptions and practices are rarely overt or intentional discrimination, but the results are, nonetheless, discriminatory. For example, on two occasions I observed a teacher asking three Latina students to stand by the door until she was done taking attendance because they had arrived to class just seconds after the bell had rung. In the previous class meetings, however, the teacher had not asked European American students to stand by the door when they arrived late. Such practices are often based on unacknowledged assumptions about race, class, gender, and age, and these assumptions shape the ways we extend respect to our students. And as students tell us, respect makes a substantial difference in their learning of both literacy and content concepts. Specifically, our respect for students shapes literacy and content learning because it influences the texts (print, visual, and audio texts included) we offer, the ways we choose to discuss or use those texts, and the ways we are able to interact with our students.

Some groups may experience more respect than others because they have the power and voice that disenfranchised groups lack. That is, parents of students in more affluent settings not only have strategies for making their voices heard, but they have the power to make sure their perspectives are valued or respected (see Tilove, 1999; Wells & Serna, 1996). Parents from lower income brackets or parents who do not speak the dominant language of the school lack both voice and power.

Cultural differences also shape teachers' abilities to respect students and the unique experiences and values students bring from outside school. Often teachers and school personnel lament parents' lack of participation in school activities, but in many cases, different cultural patterns shape how parents and families participate in school. Pacific Islanders, for example (a group well represented in Salt Lake City schools), do not encourage or expect parents to participate in their children's school lives; as a result, many Pacific Islander parents keep what they consider a respectful distance from their children's school (Tavake-Pasi, 1996), which often appears to mainstream U.S. educators to indicate a lack of respect for or interest in their children's education.

Gee, Michaels, and O'Connor (1992) also have illustrated how cultural differences shape the ways parents and children interact with their schools. Using discourse analysis, Gee et al. documented the different ways two young children told stories in their kindergarten sharing time, illustrating that an African American child told a circular story that called for interaction (such as a call and response format) and that repeated themes in a poetic, rhythmic way (see also Gee, 1996). In the same classroom a European American child told a story with a clear beginning, middle, and end, much like the story grammars taught as literacy strategies in mainstream school settings. Throughout the storytelling, the student was supported by teacher prompts. In contrast, not only did the classroom teacher react negatively to the African American child's story—telling her to sit down before she was finished—but she also subsequently identified the child as in need of special education. The child spent her next years in resource settings. The teacher was not overtly racist—she did not set out to limit the African American child's school success—but her lack of understanding of cultural and language practices other than her own served to limit the child's possibility for success. Students' and teachers' "ways with words" (Heath, 1983), constructed as people engage in everyday cultural practices, shape the respect extended to students and parents, as well as the future learning opportunities of students.

Finally, as teachers, we tend to respect the practices to which we can relate most easily. For instance, many White and middle-class teachers unconsciously tend to privilege White and middle-class practices, knowledge bases, and Discourses. Teachers of all colors and backgrounds can address these issues of understanding and respect if they strive to expand their understanding of the world and to learn about practices and Discourses that fall outside their everyday worlds. Although we cannot learn the specific values of every single student we encounter in a school year, and although we should not essentialize our students' lives in terms of culture, race, class, or gender, we can strive to better understand different cultural, community, and family practices and Discourses so that we can better respect our students. For example, Moll and his colleagues (Moll, 1994; Moll et al., 1989) have engaged teachers in studying the funds of knowledge available in their students' homes and communities. With Moll's guidance, the teachers learn how to see knowledge bases, practices, and Discourses that differ from their own as resources for teaching and learning within their classrooms. See Box 6-1 for resources that detail how teachers, parents, students, and researchers can work together to learn about community and family funds of knowledge and Discourses.

BOX 6-1
Further Reading About Community-Based Literacy Research and Teaching

Cairney, T., & Ruge, J. (1998). *Community literacy practices and schooling: Towards effective support for students*. Canberra City, ACT: Commonwealth Department of Employment, Education, Training, and Youth Affairs.

Heath, S.B. (1983). *Ways with words: Language, life, and work in communities and classrooms*. Cambridge, UK: Cambridge University Press.

McLaughlin, M.W., Irby, M.A., & Langman, J. (1994). *Urban sanctuaries: Neighborhood organizations in the lives and futures of inner-city youth*. San Francisco: Jossey-Bass.

Moll, L.C., Veléz-Ibañéz, C., & Greenberg, J. (1989). *Year one progress report: Community knowledge and classroom practice: Combining resources for literacy instruction* (IARP Subcontract L-10, Development Associates). Tucson, AZ: University of Arizona.

Noll, E. (1998). Experiencing literacy in and out of school: Case studies of two American Indian youths. *Journal of Literacy Research, 30*(2), 205–233.

Searle, C. (1998). *None but our words: Critical literacy in classroom and community*. Buckingham, UK: Open University Press.

*Reflection Point*_____

Write in your journal about the community in which you teach. What different groups are represented? How are the backgrounds of the members of these groups like yours? How are they different? With these reflections as a guide, try to collect some data. You might start by collecting demographic data about your school and community. Then try contacting a small group of parents and asking them to participate in a focus group interview about what they'd like to see happen in their children's education. During the interview, try to listen for the Discourses and funds of knowledge that they bring. After the interview, reflect on how you might incorporate these Discourses and funds of knowledge into your teaching. Think about ways that you might include the parents in this planning.

Making Content Meaningful and Interesting

I have learned a great deal about the importance of a teacher's "manner" from excellent teachers. When I refer to "manner," I speak of qualities about teachers that hook adolescents, get them interested in the content of the class, and help them see teachers as people who care about them (for more on teacher manner, see Fenstermacher, 1992; Richardson & Fallona, 1999). I also refer to qualities that help teachers make content meaningful and help them connect content to their students' lives. These qualities become evident in everyday practices that teachers often employ without specific planning, although I have noted that most successful teachers plan to conduct activities and practices that engage students in the content.

Teaching Manner

I first began to think systematically about the relation of manner, humor, and creativity when Ms. Landy used these words to describe one of the teachers who had made an impact on her thinking about teaching (Moje, 1996):

> When I applied for the Golden Apple award, or when they sent me the papers for it, they asked me about some people who influenced my life. And I thought of two in particular. One was a science teacher, a physics teacher. And he had a great sense of humor, and he tried lots of hands-on kinds of things, and a wonderful manner with the students. And the other was an English teacher who [inaudible word], he would kind of remind me of Ichabod Crane, remember the *Legend of Sleepy Hollow*? Very tall, slender, and he used to ride our bus, he was a single person. And he wasn't very active or anything, but I could always remember he smiled. And he really stimulated me to reach into my imagination with what I had read and to be creative. And, you know, those two people stand out so much in my life.

Note that Landy herself cited her model teacher's manner as an important aspect of what made her feel cared for and of what helped her learn physics and develop creativity. I observed Landy (and many other teachers) exhibiting similar qualities. For example, when teaching the concept of mole in chemistry, Landy routinely wore a T-shirt with a picture of a telephone and a mole (the animal). The T-shirt read, "Got mole problems? Call Avogadro: 6.02×10^{23}." Wearing this humorous shirt as well as other similar practices contributed to students' assessment that Landy was spontaneous and funny, thus endearing Landy to the students. But it did more than that: The content of the shirt highlighted the difference between everyday language and the language of chemistry through word play. As simple as this seems, Landy's T-shirt and her discussion of it with students represents a content literacy strategy: It emphasized the importance and uniqueness of language and knowledge in a discipline. Readers had to know what mole was about in order to really understand the pun, a point that Landy reinforced often by bringing in cartoons and comics from newspapers and magazines.

Landy wove her interest in humor into her class assignments, as well, so that her manner connected to the content. In other words, she did not just tell jokes and tease the students, but she integrated humor and humanness into science content as much as possible, as illustrated in the project she described in the following interview.

Landy: I'm gonna try, finally, my little chemtoons project. I've been having them cut out articles from the newspapers. And probably within the next two weeks I'm going to start them on that project so that just before vacation, they will have that as a presentation to make. See how they can take concepts and put them into a pictorial form. So that they convey a meaning. A scientific meaning.

Elizabeth: And will they have to come up with a joke that comes with that?

Landy: Not necessarily a joke. There are different kinds of cartoons that we have. There are editorial cartoons in the papers. There are cartoon strips. There are so many different kinds, and I think that just looking at the different types of cartooning, I've drawn some up myself so I'll share those with them. I cut a whole bunch of them out, an assortment. But each of them has an underlying scientific theme in it. So what I want them to see is that the class can pick out the theme from the picture. And this will help those students who have an artistic ability maybe shine a little bit more. They're given an opportunity to do so in a science class. It's kind of tough to summarize in a picture bunches of articles. It really is.

Elizabeth: It is, you're absolutely right. Will they—maybe I missed this from what you were saying before—are they supposed to pick a theme, and then find articles that meet that theme? Or are they just picking out articles as they go along?

Landy: What I'm having them do first is to just skim the newspapers. Go through and take a look at anything that deals with science. And then out of that collection that they gather, to choose one or two that really interest them. See we're talking about this interest thing again. It has to be of interest to them. And then to go out and provide them an opportunity to research in the library on that topic. And come up with enough information to convey, or to gather up, or to finally result in a picture, the formation of a picture that conveys some kind of concern, you know, an environmental concern or science concept.

*Reflection Point*_____

Write a description of your own manner as a teacher. Then try to observe the teaching of two other people (these may or may not be formal educators) whom students identify as great teachers (listen carefully to why students call them great, however). Try to identify the qualities that make these two people unique. How do they compare to you in terms of their manner with students? What might you change about your own manner as a result of your observations and analyses? What qualities do you already possess that you'd like to enhance?

Using Multiple Forms of Representation and Communication

Note that Landy not only brought humor into her classroom via units like the chemtoons project, but she also incorporated multiple forms of representation into her teaching in this way. When she stated that she wants them to see the scientific theme from the picture, she was teaching them that meanings can be represented in more than just print or chemical equations. She also gave students an opportunity to represent their understanding of science in multiple ways: "And this will help those students who have an artistic ability maybe shine a little bit more." Landy's words illustrate her attempts to integrate science with other disciplines and to bring science to students' everyday worlds and their everyday worlds to scientific understanding.

Similarly, Dillon and O'Brien (see Dillon, O'Brien, Moje, & Stewart, 1994) discuss the impact that Joe Ruhl, a biology teacher with whom they worked, had on his students' learning when he dressed like the monk Gregor Mendel as a way of introducing a discussion of genetics. Ruhl's performance may not have taught in-depth concepts critical to understanding genetics, but the costume drew students into the study of genetics and demonstrated another way of representing scientific work. Moreover, Ruhl illustrated that scientists can come in many disguises; anyone who investigates the natural world can contribute to scientific understanding.

Drawing from different forms of representation and communication, Diane, the English teacher with whom I worked, often told stories in class about her life both as a way of building relationships with students and encouraging them to think about ways in which the literature they were reading might connect to their lives. It is no coincidence that students were most engaged in discussions whenever Diane shared these life stories. It is also no coincidence that their reader response journals and other writings were more detailed and rich after one of Diane's stories, because her stories helped students see how they might also connect their lives to the material they were reading. As a way of encouraging students to use different forms for representing understanding, Diane at times asked students to draw or to create poetry or musical lyrics in response to novels.

Diane also used popular films as a way of visually portraying the concepts that students read about in their reading workshop. For example, when reading *The Cage* (Sender, 1988), a novel about the Holocaust, Diane showed a clip from the film *Schindler's List* to help the students form a visual representation of the ghettoes that Sender described in the novel. Following the reading of that novel, Diane showed the movie *The Long Walk Home*, about the oppression of African Americans in the United States to link the study of racism, hate, and violence to more immediate experiences in the students' lives. As they watched the movie over several class periods, they read an article about Rosa Parks's stand against oppression and the growth of the U.S. Civil Rights movement. Because the character in the film, played by Whoopi Goldberg, has to endure a painful walk home each evening as a result of the bus boycott, students had a clearer visual image of why Parks finally rebelled against discrimination.

These different reinforcements of their readings served as more than fun or engaging activities. They helped students think differently about concepts or information as they put their thinking into different forms or as they experienced concepts in print, visually, and aurally. As Eisner (1994) suggests, different forms (such as print, art, performance, music, and oral language) allow students to make different meanings. As students experience multiple representations of the same concept, they "transmediate" (Siegel, 1995). That is, they connect the many different understandings or meanings from each representation, thus resulting in a deeper understanding than they would construct from one form alone.

Reflection Point

Construct a list of multiple forms of representation that you could use to teach the central concepts of your discipline. In your list, include five resources for each of the following categories: (a) narrative texts, (b) informational or expository texts, (c) music texts, (d) movie or film texts, (e) artistic texts. If you really feel ambitious, start by generating a list of the most important concepts in your discipline, and then construct separate lists for each concept.

A teacher's engaging manner and multiple forms of representation notwithstanding, it is important to acknowledge that these qualities and practices are not always enough to connect content to real-world issues in the lives of students. In each of the classrooms described previously and in others that I have studied, students experienced varying levels of engagement and meaningfulness. As Heather, from Landy's class, told me in an interview in which we discussed wave theory, "It [wave theory] isn't about life and death." The irony of this statement is that wave theory does have implications for life and death because the theory is the basis of nuclear chemistry (for more on this, see Dillon & Moje, 1998). Thus, despite Landy's engaging manner and use of multiple forms for representing and communicating understanding, Heather saw chemistry solely as the study of matter, with few, if any, implications for her own life or the lives of others. I mention this to underscore the point that manner and multiple forms alone are not enough to make lasting and deep connections from content to students' lives. Heather indicated in several interviews that she valued Landy as a superior teacher, but Heather left chemistry with little sense of how it might be related to her life in the world outside of school. In the remaining chapters, I offer some ideas for how to weave a positive manner and multiple forms of representation into focused projects in which students inquire about, and even take action on, real-world problems and issues related to content area concepts.

Chapter 7

Toward a Secondary Literacy Pedagogy

> *Elizabeth:* *How would you make class so kids still learn some-*
> *thing, but it also was more interesting and they didn't*
> *grow to hate it?*
>
> *Jeffrey:* *Like there was that movie* Dangerous Minds.
>
> *Elizabeth:* *What—*
>
> *Jeffrey:* *That's kind, that's kind of like how she does it. 'Cause*
> *it's like, her class is like, it has lots of bad kids in it,*
> *gangs and stuff … Just like they do a project of some-*
> *thing. I'd ask, I'd ask the kids what do they like most, or*
> *what's one of the things they like to do, one that was*
> *most like, one that kids like the most, that they, that a*
> *lot of 'em agreed with. That's what I would use to do*
> *the project.*

This conversation, extracted from an interview I had with Jeffrey, gives us some insights about what might engage adolescents in learning. As one can see from Jeffrey's response, he believed that finding activities or topics in which students are most interested and asking them to do projects centered on those activities and topics would be the best way to engage young people in learning. I agree with Jeffrey, although I will expand on the specifics of his idea a bit.

In Chapter 6, I presented some general ideas about respect, manner, and multiple forms of representation that have implications for how to respond in practice to kids' insights. In this chapter I will focus on how we can change our secondary literacy teaching—indeed our secondary teaching, in general—in systematic ways in order to meet the needs and interests of many different students. As I worked with students in my last study, I realized that they needed more than specific content knowledge, literacy strategies, or encouragement to write from their experience. They needed all of these things, but they also needed a *reason* for engaging in the work, some *coherence* in the activities they were asked to do, and specific *guidance* in how to use literacy as a tool for achieving different purposes, whether cognitive, social, or political. These needs point to the importance of thinking about the construction of a coherent, planful pedagogy that has responsive teaching at its core.

The word *pedagogy* indicates that what I will offer is more than a prescribed curriculum, and it is more than a set of strategies to be used randomly or in isolation from one another. There are two steps in developing coherent, planful pedagogy. First, it seems important that we organize our teaching practices by thinking carefully about our ultimate goals for student learning, then frame our practices within a perspective—or a combination of perspectives—that help us accomplish these goals. By goals, I mean more than specific content standards or objectives. Although these are important, my research with adolescents indicates that we need to think about *what we hope to achieve when teaching these standards or objectives*. Second, we can help students construct inquiry-based projects that allow them to learn content concepts and achieve the goals we see as important for education. How one constructs projects will depend on one's ultimate goals for student learning.

Thinking About the Ultimate Purpose of Education

Educational theorists have posited different views of the ultimate purpose of education throughout history. Fenstermacher and Soltis (1998) discuss several perspectives on the purpose of education, three of which I present here: education to preserve the status quo, education to equalize imbalances in society, and education to change society.

Education to Preserve the Status Quo

Some people (whether parents, students, educators, government leaders, or business people) see education as a way to maintain or return to the *status quo* in society. Thus, literacy educators who follow this perspective would value literatures and informational texts that have been valued by dominant groups throughout the group's history. Such educators might subscribe to Hirsch, Kett, and Trefil's (1987) notion of "cultural literacy," which suggests that there are concepts to be learned and books to be read that symbolize a society's values and beliefs. These educators would be interested in ensuring that young people are able to extract information from text in order to use the information to solve problems and to contribute to the maintenance of society.

For example, when working with a student like Mark, the young African American and Hawaiian man who participated in an African drumming troupe (see Chapter 4, this volume), such educators would concentrate on teaching standard English literature and writing processes or on what are considered important historical events in U.S. history. In a world history class, Mark's knowledge of African drumming might be seen as relevant to furthering his understanding of Africa's history, but it would not be considered a significant aspect of learning about mainstream U.S. society. In terms of literacy the focus would be on Mark's comprehension and construction of standard print texts across a number of sources.

Education to Equalize Imbalances in Society

In contrast to the *status quo* perspective, others view education as a way to make people equal, so that groups that are traditionally disenfranchised can achieve as much as groups that have been powerful. Literacy educators who follow this perspective seek to offer opportunities to traditionally disenfranchised young people, opportunities that had not been available in the past. Such educators use progressive methods such as comprehension strategies, reader response, or writing process approaches to engage their students. These methods are considered progressive because they are oriented toward change. Perhaps the most well-known progressive theorist in education is John Dewey (1916), whose focus on experience-based, democratic education can be traced in many methods identified as progressive in orientation. Progressive methods provide opportunities for students to interact with one another and to learn strategies for proficient reading and writing with the goal of increasing students' skills so that they can succeed in mainstream social settings.

Progressive educators would work with Mark quite differently than would educators who wished to maintain the *status quo*. Progressive educators would be likely to bring Mark's interest in drumming into the curriculum by encouraging him to write and read about his interests. They would then use his writings and readings to teach the skills necessary to compete in mainstream society; they would focus on how to organize an essay about African drumming, for example, in a standard format, using standard punctuation and spelling.

Education to Change Society

A third perspective offers that education should ultimately serve to change society, by changing the ways all people think and act and by changing institutional structures that support oppressive or discriminatory practice. A critical or radical educator would view literacy as a *tool* for making such changes, rather than as a function necessary for success. In other words, the goal of these educators is not the production of literate persons who can either contribute economically to existing society or achieve equity for themselves in society, although they believe that youth, when equipped with various literacy tools will be able to do just that. Instead, their ultimate goal is to equip youth with the tools necessary to construct a fair, democratic, and ethical society. Such a society would be one in which people continually challenge the oppressive practices and structures that allow some people to be marginalized or excluded from opportunities for material goods and social relationships.

If these critical or radical educators worked with Mark, they might also use comprehension strategies, reader response, and writing process approaches with the African drumming knowledge that Mark brings to the classroom. However, they would encourage Mark to use his developing literacies to reposition African drumming as an important cultural and communicative practice in U.S. society. They would support Mark's inquiry about African drumming as a practice that was prohibited during slavery, and would encourage him to study other practices developed by African American people to maintain their cultural identities and relationships

Chapter 7

109

(see Kelly, in press). Educators operating from critical or radical perspectives would encourage Mark to examine—using both conventional and nonconventional literacies—why drumming as one form of communicative practice is not as highly valued as are print literacies. As part of such an inquiry, they would encourage his exploration of issues of race, class, and culture as possible explanations for the privileging of one form above another, and they would support him as he worked to reposition such practices alongside print literacies. Different beliefs about the purpose of education get expressed in teaching. Planful teaching takes into account larger issues of purpose of education, as well as issues related to disciplinary and cultural Discourses and students' needs and interests.

Pedagogical Approaches

Another way to discuss planful teaching is in terms of pedagogy. In my teaching, I have identified three particularly salient pedagogical approaches: cognitive or sociocognitive approaches, sociocultural approaches, and critical approaches.

Each of these approaches focuses on different aspects of development, with cognitive and sociocognitive approaches focusing more on the individual's development, and sociocultural and critical approaches focusing more on the development of groups. Sociocultural and critical approaches, although both group-focused, are differentiated by what educators who take these approaches hope to achieve. Sociocultural approaches draw from sociocultural theory, which argues that people learn important practices (ways of doing and knowing), processes (ways of constructing knowledge), and Discourses (ways of talking, reading, writing, moving, dressing) as they participate in groups oriented toward particular goals. Thus, sociocultural approaches emphasize group activities in which youth might learn these different practices, processes, and Discourses. Critical approaches also assume that people learn practices, processes, and Discourses as members of groups, but these approaches focus on changing oppressive practices, processes, and Discourses embodied in dominant institutional structures such as school.

These categories are representations of trends in teaching but, as with any categories, they do not and cannot represent reality. The categories provide a useful heuristic for thinking about where we each fit in terms of pedagogy, but in practice, we are likely to draw from each category at some point in our teaching. In fact, in my teaching, I use aspects of each pedagogical approach, and I use strategies that accompany each approach (see Figure 1). In other words, I have constructed a hybrid pedagogy that facilitates cognitive, cultural, and critical learning.

Figure 1
Pedagogical Approaches

Cognitively Based Pedagogy	Socioculturally Based Pedagogy	Critically Based Pedagogy
Key ideas:	*Key ideas:*	*Key ideas:*
• Learning involves "linking the new to the known."	• Learning occurs in interaction.	• Learning involves the deconstruction and reconstruction of texts, structures, and discourses.
• Learning involves the construction of knowledge.	• Learning is always situated in social, cultural, and historical contexts.	• Learning involves asking "whose interests are served" by particular ideas and practices.
• Learning is enhanced if concepts are approached according to a Before-During-After pedagogical framework.	• Learning relies on language and literacy as tools; these tools are socioculturally and historically situated.	• Learning requires that students challenge privileged or marginalized positions on the basis of physical, social, and/or economic markers.
• Pedagogy aims to provide situations in which learners can engage in physical and cognitive experiences that allow them to construct their own understandings (or to assimilate and accommodate information).	• Pedagogy aims to construct communities of practice in which learners work together to appropriate culturally useful knowledge or to generate new understandings of an experience.	• Pedagogy refuses to accept the curriculum as a given; curriculum begins with but also extends students' experiences.
• Pedagogy encourages social interaction for the purpose of challenging and reshaping knowledge constructions.	• Pedagogy is especially sensitive to different ways of knowing and being in the world.	• Pedagogy relies on language and literacy as socioculturally and institutionally situated tools for taking action in the world.

For example, for young people to take a critical perspective of the world, learning to analyze texts, discourses, and practices that reproduce stereotypes, they need certain skills to engage in such analysis. Students need to be able to comprehend, extract, and synthesize information across multiple texts, both print and nonprint. In addition, although the use of certain cognitive strategies will improve their comprehension and composition processes, they also develop both cognitively and socially as they work as members of groups, or communities of practice. They need opportunities to work together, to talk to one another, and to "apprentice" with more knowledgeable peers (see Lave & Wenger, 1991; Rogoff, 1990; Vygotsky, 1978). At the same time, however, communities of practice can overlap, so that students are never simply a member of one, neat community of practice when they are in classrooms. They bring many different identities and community affiliations with them, and at times these identities and affiliations conflict with one another, allowing for differential and sometimes oppressive relations of power to develop even within a well-developed classroom community. (For more on how peer interactions can result in conflict and in oppressive power differentials among students, see Box 7-1 on page 112.)

A strategy derived from one particular pedagogical framework can be adapted to achieve goals related to a different pedagogical approach. For example, the K-W-L strategy (What I Know, What I Want to Know, and What I Have Learned) (Ogle, 1986) can be used in a critical approach, even though it was designed to guide students before, during, and after their reading so that they could efficiently and accurately extract information from text—a more cognitive pedagogical framework. A simple way to adapt such a strategy so that students can use it to analyze texts critically is to ask students to use multiple texts on the same topic, written from different perspectives, to find "answers" to their "What I Want to Know" questions. As students find various representations of the "facts" in the different texts they examine, teachers can encourage students to ask how and why information gets represented in particular ways.

To elaborate, a history teacher could use a K-W-L strategy to introduce the concept of immigration to U.S. history students. After generating lists of what students know and want to know, the history teacher could

---

BOX 7-1
Further Reading About Power Relations In Peer Groups

To learn more about the power relations that kids experience when working within peer groups, you may want to read some of these analyses of small-group interactions:

Alvermann, D.E. (1995/1996). Peer-led discussions: Whose interests are served? *Journal of Adolescent & Adult Literacy, 39*(4), 282–289.

Evans, K.S. (1996). A closer look at literature discussion groups: The influence of gender on student response and discourse. *The New Advocate, 9*(4), 183–196.

Fassio, K.J. (1999). *The politics of young students' lives and literacy practices.* Unpublished doctoral dissertation, University of Utah, Salt Lake City, UT.

Lensmire, T. (1994). *When the children write: Critical revisions of the writing process.* New York: Teachers College Press.

Moje, E.B., & Shepardson, D.P. (1998a). Social interactions and children's changing understandings of electric circuits. In B. Guzzetti & C. Hynd (Eds.), *Theoretical perspectives on conceptual change* (pp. 17–26). Mahwah, NJ: Erlbaum.

Moje, E.B., & Shepardson, D.P. (1998b). Social interactions and children's changing understandings of electric circuits: Exploring unequal power relations in "peer"-learning groups. In B. Guzzetti & C. Hynd (Eds.), *Theoretical perspectives on conceptual change* (pp. 225–234). Mahwah, NJ: Erlbaum.

---

then distribute several texts, such as excerpts from any U.S. history textbook; from John F. Kennedy's (1964) *A Nation of Immigrants;* from Jacob Riis's photography (collected in *How the Other Half Lives* [1971]); Alex Haley's (1976) *Roots,* also available on video (Haley, 1992); Julia Alvarez's (1992) *How the Garcia Girls Lost Their Accents;* and the popular film *Titanic* (Cameron, 1997). Using the list of questions generated in the Want to Know section of the K-W-L, students could work through the multiple forms of representation (informational texts, photos, narrative text, and film) offered by the teacher to answer the questions. The various perspectives of the texts, combined with the different media used to convey meaning, provide opportunities for students to see how author background, bias, and purpose shape text meaning (comparing, for example, Kennedy's background and purpose in *A Nation of Immigrants* with Riis's background and purpose in *How the Other Half Lives*). Students can question why certain groups are portrayed in the texts while the voices and experiences of others are minimized or overlooked, as illustrated by U.S. history textbooks' focus on European immigration without mention of involuntary immigrants or of those who came to the United States as refugees or exiles. Students could compare the portrayal of immigrants in Kennedy's *A Nation of Immigrants* to that of African slaves represented in Haley's *Roots* or that of the Dominican families in Alvarez's *How the Garcia Girls Lost Their Accents*. By juxtaposing these different texts within the scaffold provided by the cognitively based K-W-L strategy, teachers give students opportunities to examine texts critically while also being guided and supported cognitively, before, during, and after their reading, viewing, or discussing activities. These critical readings do not happen on their own, of course, but they are facilitated by the use of multiple forms of multiple texts.

Reflection Point

What kind of pedagogy seems to fit best with your content area perspectives, beliefs, experiences, and goals? Why? Look back at the philosophy that you wrote while reading Chapter 2. How does your choice of pedagogical framework fit with your stated philosophy? Can you construct a lesson for your content area that represents one of the pedagogical frameworks? Can you construct a lesson that is a hybrid of the three frameworks outlined in this chapter and illustrated in Box 7-1? What would that lesson look like? Which strategies might you use in your content area to teach within your pedagogical framework?

Engaging Kids In Purposeful Learning Through Project-Based Pedagogy

Another way to achieve coherence while maintaining responsive-ness is to engage students—just as Jeffrey suggested in the conversation that opened this chapter—in inquiry-based projects about ideas, questions, and experiences of interest to them. Because students need teachers to guide and extend the inquiry they do so that they can move beyond their experiences, it is important that project-based pedagogy be framed within one of the pedagogical approaches discussed in the prior section of this chapter. One can, for example, engage in cognitively driven project-based pedagogy, or one can offer sociocultural or critical projects to students. Whatever teachers decide to offer, they must be planful, and they must move students beyond their experiences. In a continuation of my previous conversation with Jeffrey, he elaborated on his ideas.

Elizabeth: So you'd have them [students] write about something or read about it if they liked it. Like let's say they liked most to, can you think of an example of something, um, play hacky [a game known as hacky sack] or something? Would they write and read about that?

Jeffrey: Uh-huh.

Elizabeth: Okay, and then you'd use their writing and reading to teach 'em what? ...Like what kinds of things would you teach them if they were, if they said, "Well, we really like playing hacky." Then what would you do?

Jeffrey: Well then you ask 'em like, what games they like to play the most.... There's a real lot of 'em [games]. And if they say, like, "Okay, well I like such and such," then you say, "Okay, then write about that one. Write about that one, tell me what you think is so fun about it and what you like about it, and the rest of the class can learn from it."

Although Jeffrey's idea of working with things that kids like is important, it needs to be refined. Pedagogy begins with a big concept and is con-structed around a larger framework that is driven by goals, philosophies, beliefs, and values of students, teacher, and content area. As discussed in Chapters 3 and 4, students will not learn much if they only explore the things they already know how to do well. As Jeffrey suggests, if project results are shared, then students will learn from what other students study, but there is some limit to what a curriculum of hacky sack, for example, can offer to youth. Thus, project-based pedagogy should not be constructed as a free-wheeling, anything-goes pedagogy.

More specifically, in project-based pedagogy, the students generate questions around a larger concept, questions that stimulate inquiry. Project-based pedagogy begins with student experience, but teachers have the responsibility of guiding students to new levels and topics of inquiry. With teacher guidance, modeling, and the teaching of inquiry tools, students can go beyond their original, sometimes narrowly defined, questions to open new lines of inquiry. This guidance involves teaching tools for critical reading, writing, thinking, and questioning. It also involves giving students space and time to complete projects in various ways, and encouraging them to use many different kinds of texts and forms of representation. In another conversation the following year, Jeffrey described a project that he was working on in a class offered by his alternative school program:

Jeffrey: Like we're doing [a report], about where I'm from. We're like researching our ancestors and where we came from. And what are the holidays there, what do they do there.

Elizabeth: Right.

Jeffrey: All kinds of different things like that.

Elizabeth: So you're doing...

Jeffrey: What kind of government they got.

Elizabeth: That is so cool because remember that time we were talking about um, the Mexican history?

Jeffrey: Uh huh [yes].

Elizabeth: Um, you said, you know, you hadn't learned any of that, you just learned that from your Grandpa? Now are you learning stuff like that? That's cool.

Jeffrey: See like what we're doing is, we like we go to the library and get out of a encyclopedias and we get information and we write it down and then we just like do a rough draft of what we're going to do. We have to like draw the flag and stuff. Like color it and write it down. I just finished today.

> **Elizabeth:** And you did it on Mexico?
>
> **Jeffrey:** On Spain.
>
> **Elizabeth:** Spain?
>
> **Jeffrey:** Yeah.
>
> **Elizabeth:** Cool. Is your heritage more Spanish than Mexican?
>
> **Jeffrey:** No it's more Mexican than Spanish.
>
> **Elizabeth:** But you just wanted to learn more about Spain than Mexico?
>
> **Jeffrey:** Well the teacher said like, do like, if you're just all one thing [ethnicity] then just do that one thing, but if you've got like different mixes, then do them both, or three, or a multiple, whatever.
>
> **Elizabeth:** Oh so you did both?
>
> **Jeffrey:** Yeah.

In this class, Jeffrey was given a focus of inquiry and asked to make it his own by exploring experiences, customs, and values that were of interest to him. This is only one way to conceptualize project-based pedagogy; many different versions of project-based pedagogy are already in use by a number of teachers and curriculum developers across the country (see Box 7-2 for a list of reports on various project-based curricula and pedagogical approaches). While there are many different features of project-based pedagogy, some general tenets include (a) driving or authentic questions that encompass worthwhile and meaningful content anchored in real-world problems; (b) research and artifact creation that allow students to learn concepts, apply information, represent, and communicate knowledge; (c) collaboration among students, teachers, and others in the community; and (d) the use of multiple forms of representation and text, including electronic technologies (see Krajcik, Blumenfeld, Marx, Bass, & Fredericks, 1998). Drawing from critical pedagogy, and in particular, from the work of Hynds (1997), I add a fifth feature to this list: the development of critical, social awareness and the ability to take action against discriminatory practices in society.

As suggested previously, project-based pedagogy does not mean that anything goes, that any question, any problem, or any concept should form the basis of the project. In each discipline particular concepts are

critical concepts in content area

BOX 7-2
Further Reading About Project-Based Pedagogies

For more on project-based pedagogies in different content areas, you might want to read some of these materials:

Guthrie, J.T., & McCann, A.D. (1997). Characteristics of classrooms that promote motivations and strategies for learning. In J.T. Guthrie & A. Wigfield (Eds.), *Reading engagement: Motivating readers through integrated instruction* (pp. 128–14). Newark, DE: International Reading Association.

Guthrie, J.T., Van Meter, P., McCann, A., Wigfield, A., Bennett, L., Poundstone, C., Rice, M.E., Faibisch, F., Hunt, B., & Mitchell, A. (1996). Growth of literacy engagement: Changes in motivations and strategies during concept-oriented reading instruction. *Reading Research Quarterly, 31*(3), 305–325.

Marx, R.W., Blumenfeld, P.C., Krajcik, J.S., & Soloway, E. (1997). Enacting project-based science. *The Elementary School Journal, 97*(4), 341–358.

Mercado, C.I. (1992). Researching research: A classroom-based student-teacher-researchers collaborative project. In A.N. Ambert & M.D. Alvarez (Eds.), *Puerto Rican children on the mainland: Interdisciplinary perspectives* (pp. 167–192). New York: Garland.

Merino, B.J., & Hammond, L. (1998). Family gardens and solar ovens: Making science education accessible to culturally and linguistically diverse students. *Multicultural Education, 5*(3), 34–37.

Moje, E.B. (1999). From expression to dialogue: A study of social-action literacy projects in an urban school setting. *Urban Review, 31*, 305–330.

Moll, L.C., & Gonzalez, N. (1994). Lessons from research with language minority children. *Journal of Reading Behavior, 26*, 439–456.

Rosebery, A.S., & Warren, B. (Eds.). (1998). *Boats, balloons, and classroom video: Science teaching as inquiry*. Portsmouth, NH: Heinemann.

Warren, B., Rosebery, A.S., & Conant, F.R. (1989). *Cheche Konnen: Science and literacy in language minority classrooms* (Report No. 7305). Cambridge, MA: Bolt, Beranek, & Newman.

---

considered important for students to learn. Teachers can help students frame potential lines of inquiry within specific concepts. Start by identifying the most critical concepts in the discipline (for help with this task, consult the national standards for the content area). For example, when teaching biology, I wanted to be sure that students learned about what life was and about the many forms of life, so I first divided the year into an exploration of different life forms. From there, I developed questions to prompt students' thinking, questions such as: What makes something alive? and What are the different kinds of life? How are they alike? How are they different? We would then pinpoint topics for study within the different conceptual areas of biology (such as the study of plant life, animal life, protozoan life) and begin projects from these inquiry points. By consulting national or local curriculum standards, a teacher can feel confident that he or she is addressing concepts deemed important in our society, while also providing a space for students to explore areas of interest to them and offering opportunities for students to question the ideas and knowledge bases of each content area.

*Reflection Point*_____

IRP
Reading 44.

Consult state or national standards for learning in your content area, then make a list of the most important concepts in your area. If you had to choose the four most important concepts for your area and your grade level, which four would you choose? Choosing four conceptual foci will allow you to plan for 9-week projects, which give students approximately 6 weeks to complete and 2 weeks to present, and give you 1 week to evaluate. Now make a list of the skills or practices that are important to your content area (for instance, in mathematics, the ability to estimate and problem solve is important; in history, the ability to read from and for multiple perspectives is critical). How are these skills embedded in the concepts that you deem important? In what ways do the skills require or depend on conceptual understanding?

_____

"I Don't Know Why They're Teaching Us That": Problematizing Project-Based Pedagogy

As enthusiastic as I am about the potential for project-based pedagogy, my experiences with using projects in the past remind me to offer
some caveats regarding their success in classrooms, especially in classrooms in which using projects will represent a major innovation. Recall
the French class that I studied with Jayne Brozo and Bill Haas (Moje et
al., 1994). Jayne, Bill, and I struggled to maintain students' enthusiasm as
they engaged in the project pedagogy. We determined that lack of structure and their fledgling relationship with Jayne contributed to the students' frustration with the projects (see Moje et al., 1994). Similarly, Chile
attributed her failure to complete a year-long project in her ninth-grade
geography class to a lack of direction and guidance and to the length of
the project. She repeatedly commented that she was sick of working on
it although she had initially found it interesting.

Much of what we learned in the French class was reflected in the social action projects that Diane, her students, and I conducted in the context of the writer's workshop. However, we learned that even with new
pedagogy, many of the students' values and beliefs about the purpose of
schooling were not changed overnight, or even over the course of a term,
despite our use of well-structured, carefully articulated projects. Many
students resisted the project, as well. The group who studied drunk driving as a social issue in Diane's classroom, for example, wrote in their rationale that they chose to study this topic so that they "could get a good
grade." (It is interesting to note that these were two of the most academically successful students in the class.) Although their final product was
well done, they resisted working on the project until a few weeks before
their project presentation.

Resistance is not the only problem associated with project-based pedagogy: As I indicate in the next chapter, some students remained unen-
gaged when we used project-based pedagogy in the writer's workshop
class. Morever, students' social action projects were not all of high quality, and we failed to achieve some of our goals for deep and lasting critical
literacy. I interviewed students who failed to see a purpose even in pro-

ject work, as indicated in this excerpt of another conversation with Alex and Anthony, when I asked them what could be done to improve school:

Alex: [Teachers need to] give you enough time to actually do your work. Not so many projects.

Anthony: No big projects.

Elizabeth: No big projects? You did a big project in our class. I thought you liked it.

Anthony: But in history we did like 50 of'em.

Elizabeth: 50 of 'em?

Anthony: Yeah, one after another.

Elizabeth: Tell me an example of one of 'em.

Anthony: History project.

Elizabeth: What was it?

Anthony: Like the same thing but you'd look up information about inventors. And like, somethin' about political stuff.

Elizabeth: Like to get you to understand the politics of something?

Anthony: Yeah. I don't know why they're teachin' us that.

Elizabeth: Hmmm, why do you think? Why might they want you to understand politics?

Anthony: I don't know. Maybe they want me to vote.

Elizabeth: Yeah, that might be.

Anthony's failure to understand "why they're teachin' us that" suggests that simply doing projects is not enough. Even as enthusiastic as Jeffrey was about his Mexican/Spanish heritage project during his eighth-grade year, when I asked him about the project at the beginning of the next year, he responded, "I hardly remember anything about that."

Projects, then, are not panaceas. They do not promise perfect learning, but they do hold promise for improving the education of all students simply by engaging them in something meaningful, something drawn from their experiences, and something that pushes them beyond those experiences. When enacting project-based pedagogy, we need to seek ways to refine and expand the pedagogy, to teach lasting literacy and language skills while also teaching important content concepts.

*Reflection Point*_____

Write about something innovative that you would like to try in your classroom. Now think about your students: What demands does this work place on students? What new practices might they need to learn to engage wholeheartedly in the work? Who would value this work and become highly engaged in it? Who might resist engaging in the work? Does this innovation meet the needs of diverse groups of learners? Whose needs and interests might not be met? What might you do to encourage participation and engagement on the part of all students?

Interdisciplinary Project-Based Pedagogy

One possibility for making projects more meaningful for students is to engage them in project work across disciplines. When constructing interdisciplinary curricula, teams of teachers work together to bring discipline-based perspectives and discourses to bear on a central concept. For example, a team that includes history, earth science, physics, Spanish and English teachers could develop a unit around the concept of truth, asking as the driving questions of the unit projects, "What is truth in history?" "What is truth in science?" "How is language used to generate particular truths?" In each content area, the teachers and students would have opportunities to explore questions of truth in relation to the discipline being studied. Students could learn to examine claims made by authors, historians, and scientists by examining the information on which the claims are based, the positions and biases of the claimants, and the social and political climate of the times in which claims have been made. The plan calls for students to learn content concepts that are considered important to each discipline, but they should learn these concepts in a framework that connects their learning from one disciplinary community to the next. In this way, they learn more than just content-based facts; they also learn how ideas can be shaped by different disciplinary perspectives, and they learn more explicitly the differences and similarities among the disciplines.

An interdisciplinary project, then, contributes to establishing a sense of purpose by helping to build coherence across content concepts, thereby eliminating redundancy across the content areas. Interdisciplinary units can also challenge the marginalization of some content areas. Traditionally, disciplines such as science, language, social studies, and mathematics have assumed a more central position in secondary education, while disciplines such as music, physical education, foreign language, and visual and performing arts are often relegated to the margins. Interdisciplinary curricula can bring disciplines together so that they support and extend one another, rather than vie for position and power within the secondary institution (see Ball & Lacey, 1984).

Several of the teacher education students in my classes have developed examples of inclusive interdisciplinary units around central concepts important to each discipline. For example, in a collaboration among English, French, biology, and physical education teachers, the central concept could be the human body. The driving question would be "How are bodies represented and shaped in society?" Students could read literature such as *Dr. Jekyll and Mr. Hyde* (Stevenson, 1886), linking Dr. Jekyll's use of body-altering chemicals to the use of steroids among athletes. While engaged in such reading and discussion, students would learn the anatomy and physiology of muscles in biology, while also exploring healthy ways to tone and care for one's body in physical education. In the French class, students would learn French vocabulary to use in biological and physical education Discourses, to study how bodies are represented in French and U.S. cultures, and to develop their French language skills in order to read, write, and discuss body issues.

In another example, a unit plan that focused on teaching students how to take action asked students to conduct research on physical education and recreation, then write letters to support keeping physical education as part of the secondary school curriculum. In their history class, the students would learn about historical attempts to make change through social action, and in their English classes, students would learn necessary research and literacy skills for carrying out their projects and taking action to make change.

Reflection Point

Try to find at least one other teacher from another discipline with whom you could pilot an interdisciplinary project. You'll need to have students in common, and you'll need to have a common planning time to really make this work. Plan and implement one small-scale project. Try videotaping and analyzing the processes that your students follow. The rubric in Box 7-3 provides some ideas about how to start planning an interdisciplinary, project-based unit.

BOX 7-3
Questions for Developing Planful Pedagogy

Look back at the list of concepts you targeted as important to your content area.

- How might other content areas explore some aspect of the same concepts?
- What connections do you see between the concepts in your content area and the ways such concepts are addressed in other content areas?
- What are some of the goals you can set as a cross-curricular team?
- What are some of the goals you want to set for your specific content area?
- What are some of the activities you might use to achieve these goals with your students?
- What are some strategies you could use to achieve these goals with your students?
- In what ways will literacy play a part in these activities?
- How long do you think this unit will take to teach? How many lessons will you need?
- What special time considerations or constraints will you need to take into account to enact your cross-curricular unit?
- What kinds of materials will you need to teach your unit?
- How will you ensure that your unit is really a team effort among teachers?
- How will you ensure that your students see the unit as a cross-curricular approach?
- What are some innovative ways that you could assess what students have learned from this unit?
- What other concerns or considerations can you think of as you begin to plan?

With some guidance, both from me and from an examination of national and state standards, the teacher education students who have developed these units in groups have quickly found common themes across their disciplines. The greatest challenge in constructing and implementing such units occurs when disciplinary Discourses—those ways of knowing, being, acting, reading, and writing in the different disciplines—clash. But until we, as teachers, learn to work through these differences, our students will not be able to learn from us how to navigate many different Discourse communities. And it is critical that we start doing a better job of teaching our students how to work across different communities (whether professional, social, disciplinary, or cultural) because we are moving quickly into what Hall (1995) calls "new times," in which electronic technologies and other fast-paced information systems have changed the face of the world and work. Geographic distances are minimized, for example, by Internet technologies; business and industries are calling for workers to share in decision making, to navigate multiple information systems and communities of information producers, and to deliver information as a product. People are expected to engage in these practices quickly; competition is heightened in an era where life- or business-changing decisions can be made in a matter of hours. In these new times, young people need to be educated to manage a great deal of information, to work with diverse groups, and to think critically about the ways that information is constructed, transmitted, and used in society. Each of these skills requires the ability not only to cross discourse communities, but also to recognize them and to think about the different tools that are needed for participating in or changing discourse communities. As a result, interdisciplinary projects hold even more promise than just single-subject projects for making school learning meaningful for life in the everyday world.

Service Learning and Projects

A final possibility for increasing the meaningfulness of project pedagogy is service or community-based learning. Again, because we live in new times in which boundaries are breaking down more and more (except, it seems, the boundary between school and community), we need to work harder than ever to integrate students' learning *in* schools and classrooms with their lives *outside* of schools and classrooms. Together with two large research centers at the University of Michigan (The Center for Learning Technologies in Urban Schools and the Center for the Study of Early Reading Achievement), I am working in predominantly Latino/a schools and communities of southwest Detroit to add a community-based component to the project-based science curriculum being enacted by teachers in several middle schools. The project-based curricula revolve around a number of science topics, including air and water quality in the community, the physical principles that support the wearing of bike helmets, the physical principles involved in building big things like sky-scrapers and bridges, and the epidemiology of the HIV/AIDS virus. Each of these topics is intended to encompass one or more larger science concepts and is also intended to serve as the basis of a driving question or focus of inquiry that students will find authentic and engaging, such as "What is the quality of water in our river?"

Last year, in the project in which seventh graders studied the quality of air in their community, our teaching and research group—comprised of teachers, curriculum developers, and researchers—asked students to develop end-of-unit presentations that went beyond the typical reading of a written report to the class. One group prepared a local newscast in which they role-played interviews of people on the street and in homes and dramatized news reports about air-related issues. For the upcoming year, we are working on developing this project further by having the entire class prepare an actual newscast. Instead of having members of the class take on such roles as *person on the street*, we have decided to have students actually interview randomly selected community members on film, in much the same manner as the on-the-street interview so often seen on television news. We will also have students conduct scheduled interviews with business and industry leaders (whose companies or plants may be hindered by various environmental legislative acts), environmental activists, politicians, and community organization leaders.

Class members will play roles similar to those occupied by members of a news organization—reporters, data analysts, camera technicians, writers, anchors, directors, and producers. The students will be required to consult multiple sources (people, print texts, the Internet, other electronic media) and to use multiple forms of representation (print, video, audio, and graphics). In all of this work, we will continually remind students that because they are producing information that may shape viewers' knowledge and beliefs about environmental and industrial issues, they must base their research on careful scientific research (always tying the information to the science that they have learned), and they must always present the research in carefully constructed, easy-to-access forms. We'll also lead discussions with them on what it means to report the *truth* about a situation. We will ask students to think about whose truth is being reported, to whom students might owe something as they report on the issues, and how that allegiance shapes what students are willing to say and do as information gatherers and reporters.

Because we are working with predominantly Latino/a communities in bilingual immersion and second-language schools, we will encourage students to use a mixture of Spanish and English, as a way of illustrating how bi- or multilingualism can add to understanding and meaning making rather than detract from it. We will also endeavor to facilitate students' contact with as many Latino/a community members and leaders as possible, so that they can interact with members of their ethnic communities about science issues and concerns.

Audience is an important part of any authentic community and project-based approach. Our goal is to arrange to broadcast this production on a local community access channel so that community members can witness the work that the young people of their communities engage in as part of their school lives. We also feel that an actual community broadcast would give more meaning to the students' work. If we find that a community broadcast is not possible, we will endeavor to arrange for a school and community event in which the video is shown and students are on hand to answer questions about the process of making the newscast.

This work will be facilitated by an existing community-based group of parents, teachers, university workers, students, politicians, and business people who care deeply about the development and success of the young people in their community. Such groups are common in communities, and they can provide enormous support to teachers who want to extend schoolwork into the community and the community into schoolwork. I urge teachers and administrators interested in developing this kind of community-school partnership to start by contacting groups such as this one. Of the 150 to 180 students secondary school teachers meet each day, a large number have parents who are already actively involved in such groups. If you are interested in pursuing this kind of work, begin by talking to parents about ways that you can work together to make better connections between content area teaching and the students' communities. Such work requires an extensive time and energy commitment on the part of teachers, parents, and students, but it can give a real purpose to literacy and content learning in students' lives.

These ideas for interdisciplinary and community-based projects are still in development. In the next and final chapter, however, I illustrate what it looks like to put a form of project-based pedagogy into practice in one classroom. The projects represented in the next chapter were designed to focus on building social awareness and action among the students in Diane Wilson's seventh-grade English classroom.

Chapter 8

Easy to Talk About, Harder to Do: Exploring Projects in Practice

While Elizabeth chats with a few students in the back of the room, Diane begins to hand out packets of blue paper to students. Elizabeth knows what's up, but the students look at the packets quizzically. Once everyone has a packet, Diane takes her stool at the front of the room and starts to talk with the group:

"Okay! We started a couple of weeks ago on getting you guys at least started thinking about these group projects. Now is the time for serious starting on the group projects. Just so that you know, with deadlines and stuff, this fourth term, your two big things are going to be this project and reading one more novel. That's where we're going to spend our time, and that's where evaluation and grading is going to come from. So, in other words, writer's workshop, writing your own personal pieces— we won't be spending time on that anymore."

To illustrate what project-based pedagogy looks like in practice, this chapter will highlight the small-group, social action projects in which Diane, her students, and I engaged as part of the seventh-grade literacy workshop. Diane and I identified our projects as "social action projects" (despite the fact that most of our students never actually took action) because our goals for students working on the projects were (a) to identify problems or issues in society or their communities, and (b) to conduct research on these problems and issues. We hoped that the stu-

dents' inquiry would accomplish two larger goals in alignment with critically based pedagogy (as described in Chapter 7, this volume). First, we
wanted to encourage students to be conscious of how their experiences
are shaped by their relationships with others and by systems that support differential treatment based on racial, ethnic, gender, or class identities. Second, we hoped to help students develop strategies for thinking
and taking action in order to address the issues they identified in their
projects. These strategies could include the use of conventional and nonconventional literacies.

We planned the projects to help students practice the necessary literacy skills and practices for conducting research, for developing social
awareness, and for taking social action. So although we were committed
to critical or radical pedagogical goals, we incorporated aspects of cognitive and sociocultural pedagogies into our teaching. Specifically, we were
interested in providing students with experience and guidance in negotiating and synthesizing information across multiple texts and resources, as
well as in negotiating meanings among other students in collaborative relationships (for more ideas on how to support these practices in students,
consult the pieces on project-based pedagogy listed in Box 7-2 on page
117). We also wanted them to practice communicating the ideas they had
gained from research. The sociocultural aspects of our work included conducting the research as members of a whole-class community and as
members of smaller teams. In addition, we hoped that our students would
learn about being members of larger communities by interviewing and interacting with family members, other teachers, students, administrators,
local officials, community leaders, and business and industry leaders.

As indicated in the Project Components guidelines that we distributed
to students (see Appendix B), we asked student groups to prepare written
as well as oral presentations of the social action projects. We referred to the
presentations that groups would make as "performances," because we
wanted to encourage students to explore many different ways of representing and communicating their ideas, including music, art, and dramatic performance. For both the written and oral components of the project,
students were to generate a group rationale, a group description of their
process, a group explanation of what they learned, and a group assessment
of "what the project made us feel about ourselves, our friends/family, our

school, our community, our lives." Each of these components was critical to the success of the social and critical pedagogy, but the final assessment was the most important to move the students from an individualistic stance to one in which they explored as a group the implications of their research for their lives, their community, and their families. Both Diane and I engaged in a project (Diane worked collaboratively with a student, but I did not) and modeled the processes through which we moved with a succession of minilessons. Diane studied important people in her life, and I studied a social issue—beauty and body image.

In the following section, I show how we (a) introduced the idea, (b) helped students frame and reframe problems, (c) modeled the inquiry and writing of projects, and (d) modeled the performances that we wanted students to make of each of their projects. Interspersed throughout the vignettes are my reflections on the various principles of project work that are illustrated in (or in some cases missing from) the vignettes. Although these vignettes are drawn from data and include some excerpts of verbatim transcripts, the transcripts in their entirety are not included because they are so long. (If interested in reading more of the data and more analyses of the data, consult Moje [1999] or Moje and Fassio [1997]). It is important to acknowledge that we did not view these as perfect projects, but rather as an important first attempt to engage students in meaningful, sustained inquiry about questions of interest to them.

*Reflection Point*_____

Before you read on, take a minute to think about how you would introduce the projects that you planned as you read Chapter 7. What driving questions would you use to frame the inquiry that you would ask students to engage in? How much freedom would you give students in defining their own inquiry? How would you explain to them what you would be doing for the next several weeks or months? What kinds of structures would you put in place to guide and support their work? Try to address each of these questions in the plan that you began to construct as you read Chapter 8.

Introducing Social Action Projects in English Class

> Now, at the top there, it says,"For this project you will choose from two general themes: important people in my life or problems or issues in the community, society, nation, and/or world."Is there any group who has not decided, at least generally, which of those they're gonna do?
>
> Diane

To help the students plan and carry out their research and project performances, Diane and I introduced two large-scale themes, as represented in the previous quote. As a class we then brainstormed possible topics within those two themes. To get students started, we told them about the projects that we were doing, and we mentioned issues that some of them had written about during writer's workshop (for example, one student wrote an essay on pollution) and suggested that they might use the projects to develop inquiry around these issues. We then asked students to form groups and to discuss possible topics. The next step of project preparation was to distribute and discuss guidelines of project components and assessment criteria for the project (see Appendixes A and B).

To help the students think about managing their time and organizing their resources, we required each group member to keep a progress log and planning sheet (see Figures 2 and 3 on page 132). We provided the planning sheet to assist students in integrating written text with other forms of representation. Students included drawings on their planning sheets and, as they reached the final stages of the project, included the actual text that they would read or perform.

We knew that doing projects would be difficult for students after 27 weeks of writer's workshop in which they wrote personal experience essays or fictional stories. Although they had worked in groups when they conducted peer conferences over a piece of writing, their work was always directed toward revising an individual's work. The writer's workshop, as conceived traditionally, does not focus on the development of collaborative pieces. As a result, our students had learned to give and take constructive criticism about a piece of writing, but not how to negotiate different ideas that they might all bring to the same piece. We decided to

Figure 2
Sample Progress Log

Date	Work Completed	Next Steps
3-19	chose groups and topic	brainstorm about topic
3-20	got together with Mike and Elizabeth and talked about gangs	focus questions
3-21	absent	
3-22	more brainstorming	start to write a rationale
3-25	rough draft of rationale	write more
3-26		
3-27	Ms. W. taught about interviewing	write interview questions
3-28	interviewed Vance	write information down to make it a story about Vance
3-29	worked on gang project more	collect pictures of tagging and books about tagging and graffiti
4-8	started making posters	get some books about graffiti and gangs

Figure 3
Sample Planning Sheet

Video/Slide/Photo/Music	Dialogue/Narration	Props Required
Poster of common graffiti signs	Explain signs; explain why gangs use these signs	Poster board, drawings, photos
Drawings of guns and other weapons	Tell about gang violence and why gangs kill each other	Poster board, drawings

give students a great deal of background and support for generating project ideas and for conducting their inquiry. This first vignette illustrates how Diane introduced the projects to the class:

> From her stool, Diane began to work through the blue packet with students, emphasizing points she thought they might struggle with. She started with the idea that students needed to collaborate:
>
> "You will work collaboratively in small groups. Guys, collaboration means teamwork. That means you are working together, sharing ideas, everybody does his or her part...okay? There will not be any, at the end of the term, saying, "Well, he didn't do anything. It's not my fault." In a group, if you've got four people and one person does *everything* and the other three people don't do anything, the person who does everything is just as much at fault for letting that happen as the other three. Don't let that happen to you. This is a group effort, it needs to be everybody participates equally. Okay?"
>
> After emphasizing collaboration, Diane moved on to discuss the content component of the projects:
>
> "Is the content well organized and clear to others? Did you put it together so that it's...sensible. Does the paper make sense, in other words. Does the presentation make sense? Is the information accurate? So, in other words, you can't just invent a bunch of facts. If you're doing drunk driving, a group from third period's gonna do drunk driving, you can't just make up a bunch of facts. You need to research, talk to people, do some reading, do some time in the library, do some interviewing time, okay, watch news reports, whatever, to get your facts accurate."

Diane and I felt it would be important to help students think about the content for several reasons. First, the idea of identifying a problem or question and then doing research on it was new to students, at least in our setting. They did not have much experience in our class with gathering ideas from many different sources and synthesizing them in a written piece. Second, we were asking students to choose issues that they cared about, but we did not want them to remain at the level of personal knowledge in their reports. We wanted each group to start with personal knowledge and experience, then to expand that knowledge through a variety of data-gathering activities. Third, we encouraged students to use multiple forms of representation (video, music, interviews, skits, guest speakers), and we were concerned that they would put their efforts into making exciting or slick representations without making sure that the representations communicated deep content knowledge or information. One missing piece in our introduction, however, was an emphasis on how they might use some of the organization strategies we had taught throughout the year (concept mapping, category charts, etc.) to organize both their process and their information. Throughout the term, we reminded students of these strategies or taught new ones as needed, but in hindsight we wish that we had organized a series of mini-lessons on strategies to help students organize and communicate the information they collected.

In the next several minutes of the class session, Diane continued through the packet, focusing on the assessment criteria. She commented on each point about quality, neatness, preparation, presence during the performance, individuality, and collaboration. As Diane talked about each point, she gave clear, explicit instructions—including examples—that provided guidance but did not shut down possibilities for creativity. This is an important aspect of project work, especially when project work is new to students. As Bill Brozo, Jayne Haas, and I learned (see Moje et al., 1994), even high academic achievers can become frustrated if they do not have a clear sense of what is expected of them. In fact, as illustrated by Mike and Kevin in Chapter 5, successful students often have learned to be successful by following strict guidelines; students are not often rewarded for creativity and originality in school. As a result, many have learned to be rather standardized in their approach to schoolwork. Those students need even more support in project work. They need to have a structure to follow, but they also need to be nudged into more creative and challenging paths.

Our reflections on the assessment criteria suggest that it would be important to involve the students in the construction of the rubric in future iterations of the projects. Specifically, we would offer the same major categories that we used for this project, but we would ask the students to help us define what each of those categories meant. We would ask, for example, what it means to talk about the *quality* or the *originality* of a project. In this way, we could have incorporated what we had taught in literacy workshop minilessons throughout the year into the project work. Moreover, students would have a better sense of what high quality work was if they had to construct their own definitions of quality.

After going through the qualities upon which students would be evaluated, Diane went on to discuss the writing of the rationale, which we saw as a defining aspect of the project. We believed that if the students could not identify why they were studying the topic—whether important people in their lives or social problems—then they would have a hard time engaging in sustained inquiry. Helping students think through their rationales by modeling our own rationale construction was, in many ways, the first step in helping students frame problems for inquiry:

Diane: Rationale. The rationale, guys, means, "Why did we do this? What meaning does it have?" Okay? Some people in third period were talking about doing a [project on] drunk driving. Which is great, there's a lot of stuff to learn and a lot of information and a lot of study that can be done about drunk driving. But my impression was that they wanted to do drunk driving so that they could make a video of cars crashing. Well, fine, as long as that's not all it is. There needs to be some reason, some learning, something that comes from watching these cars crash. So there needs to be more to it than that. Now, Elizabeth talked in third period about her rationale, with her body imaging and things that we get from the media, she had a personal reason for doing that. Elizabeth, why don't you tell 'em what your rationale is for doing yours?

Elizabeth: Just, you know, as a kid, that I had been shaped by what I saw on TV and Barbie, and all of that kind of stuff, to try to look a particular way. So my personal rationale is that that affected me when I was growing up, and I think it probably affects all of you, so it's a way of talking about it and raising awareness. So that's my personal rationale.

Diane: So you need to have some underlying reason. So her rationale is not ,"I was hoping to spend some time looking through magazines, and I can now get a grade for it." That's not her rationale…. In other words, guys, there needs to be, if you're doing gangs, I don't want just a book of graffiti. I want "What about it? What do the people creating the graffiti think? What do the other members of society think? What does law enforcement think? What do kids think? What do adults think? What do teachers think? What does everyday Joe-guy-on-the-street think?

And what do we as a society learn from that? "In other words, guys, there needs to be some meat behind this, and not just a video of graffiti.

In a responsive, planful pedagogy, teachers invite students to construct the pedagogy with them, but also to provide experiences to challenge and extend students as well as structures to guide and focus students. Project-based pedagogy works well to achieve both responsiveness and planfulness because teachers can provide a framework for engaging in questions of interest to students, while also teaching students important new content and new skills. Note how Diane used my example as a way to encourage students to develop their interests beyond just something fun to do. She pushed them to give reasons for their inquiry and ultimately to provide the audience with rich content that would be meaningful for them. Helping students learn how to take something of interest to them and make it interesting to others was an important objective for us. We knew, however, that they would need more than this pep talk at the beginning of the term. For example, we knew that students would need to develop research skills such as the ability to locate and synthesize information across multiple texts and the ability to interview people and analyze their responses, and we knew that we would have to teach students these skills in a series of whole-class minilessons as well as in small-group interactions. Although we did not teach interviewing process until a later lesson, Diane introduced the importance of good interviewing skills in this introduction to the projects:

Diane:	Elizabeth's gonna work with you guys next week on how to conduct an interview with somebody, and you'll interview each other, so that when you go out into the community to interview people, you'll know what you're doing 'cause it's not just a matter of sticking a mic in their face and saying "What do you think?" That's one problem that I thought some of these kids did when they did their history thing here. Two girls came in to interview me about what I thought about the recent ACLU lawsuit against Northwest High.
Kara:	I saw you. Is that what you were doing?
Diane:	Well, it was kind of hard, I ended up, well, I guess it was okay the way they edited it, but I sounded like an idiot because number one, they gave me no chance to prepare,

they just walked in and said, "Can we interview you?"And they asked like this totally loaded question, which I had to sit and qualify, and…fill in their blanks for them, so that I didn't look like some sort of racist. You know, they just stuck a mic in my face. You can't do that. Elizabeth's gonna teach you about how to interview people so that you can get some, accurate responses.

After emphasizing the need for good interviewing skills, Diane moved on to discuss the importance of an oral as well as written discussion of what students would learn by engaging in the projects. Her comments also helped to connect the content concepts (both knowledge of literacy processes and specific knowledges about each social problem or personal relationship) and habits of mind (critical awareness and social action) that would be learned to everyday practices and relationships. She told a story about how her project had made her see her father differently:

Diane: Then the oral presentation, you've got to have an introduction and conclusion. Might be written, but it also might be an introduction or conclusion right in your video or in your slide presentation. It tells why you did the project, how you did it, what you learned, and what it made you feel about yourself, friends, family, school, community, and life. I know that with mine, I'm [researching] the important people in my life, I've already changed some feelings about my family that I had 'cause I went home about a week ago, and my mom had this picture of my father as a little kid. He was probably 4 years old, and he is the cutest little thing. Big ol' ears, sticking out. Blond hair, and he's standing out in the middle of this lettuce patch or something, my dad had told me a lot of stories about him as a little kid, but I'd never thought of the fact that here is this grown, 75-year-old man, as a little tiny child. And it was so cool to see this picture of him. And that kind of changed my feeling about my dad, making him just that much more human. So [your presentation will show] what did you learn, how did your feelings, how did your opinions change?

Finally, Diane ended the introduction by emphasizing the importance of using multiple forms of representation. In this case, Diane emphasized the use of multiple texts and forms of representation as a way to be creative in order to make the performances interesting, but we also envisioned multiple text and forms as important tools that students could use to represent different kinds of understanding, knowledge, and practice. We saw these tools as more than just gimmicks to liven up the performances, but many students struggled to make these other forms an integral part of their projects, something that deepened the meaning of the message. Each group, however, dove into the production of other forms of representation with enthusiasm, incorporating a great deal of material from popular cultural texts of interest to them. We saw graffiti posters, photographs, and film clips; heard music and audiotapes of interviews; and watched skits and simulations of car accidents. One group, in a particularly well-integrated use of their representational form, produced a talk-show style video on bullies.

Modeling Processes, Practices, and Tools

Teaching the Data Collection Process

To support students as they worked throughout the 2 months dedicated to projects (we also read a class novel during this time, so not every class period was completely devoted to project work), we engaged in various minilessons to model particular processes, practices, and tools. For example, because Diane and I knew that some of the students' research would involve interviewing various sources, we led the students in an interviewing activity in which they were asked to interview an assigned partner for the purpose of writing a biography (see the description of a biography writing project in Chapter 4). We worked carefully with students on generating interview questions for their group projects. We helped them refine questions and reminded them that often the way one asks a question can shape the response. We also encouraged students to think about how questions or other data-collection activities might make people feel.

For example, the group who studied homelessness wanted to take photographs of homeless people around Salt Lake City. To dissuade them from what we considered a potentially offensive act, we asked them to consider two points: First, how would they feel if someone came up and took their pictures on the street. Would they be frightened, offended, angry? If the person taking the picture asked permission first, what would they say? Would asking permission or explaining purpose be enough to take away their anger or hurt? Second, would it be appropriate for the students to ask homeless people if they could take pictures so that other people can see what it is like to be homeless? How might that make people feel? What would be the benefits and drawbacks of such an approach? We wanted our students to know that although this could be a useful research strategy in certain cases (journalism, sociological studies), there were also certain dangers and drawbacks. From this conversation, the group members decided to use different methods of collecting data. They interviewed people, they visited homeless shelters, they read books, but they did not engage in what might be offensive, problematic, or unsafe research activities. Diane and I engaged in similar conversations on a group-by-group basis. Looking back, we believe that some of these conversations could have been useful whole-class minilessons from which each group could have learned. We would do this differently in the future, perhaps engaging in spontaneous minilessons as students asked questions, but also planning some minilessons based on questions that students asked us each day.

Writing Rationales

As we worked with students in their groups, we quickly realized that although they had identified topics, students struggled to frame problems for inquiry within those topics. We were not surprised, because many teachers and researchers who use project-based pedagogy have found this to be a common problem (see Krajcik et al., 1998). Consequently, we had planned to write our own rationales and to model the process of revising them with a peer, much as we had done in the writer's workshop.

For the minilesson, Diane and I each wrote short rationales and made overhead transparencies of the actual pages so that we could show the class how we would revise with the help of a peer. Then Diane read her rationale aloud to the class, while projecting it on the screen. As she read, she made small revisions and did some sentence-level editing. I gave her feedback, and she made notes about where to expand her ideas, where to tighten or clarify text, and where to delete text. When I put my three-page, typewritten rationale on the overhead projector (see Appendix C for an edited version), the students gave a large, choral gasp. "What's wrong?" I asked, puzzled. "It's so long!" exclaimed Katie.

At that moment I was reminded of how much guidance our students would need to complete these broad, unwieldy projects. My written rationale, which had taken me at most 20 minutes to produce in a stream-of-consciousness mode the night before, represented a major piece of writing to these young writers. They were intimidated by the length of what I had written. I knew that we would have to spend much time helping them to frame their problems, identify and write their rationales for studying these problems, prepare written presentations, and give performances that represented their learning and communicated new knowledge to others. Now I was intimidated!

Nevertheless, as a class we worked through my rationale in much the same fashion that we had gone through Diane's, and then we asked kids to spend the rest of the period (about 20 minutes) drafting their rationales both individually and in groups. We walked around the room and helped them refine their work. Some students did it on their own, as Mike did; when he and Anthony read aloud their rationale for studying gang violence, graffiti, and tagging, Mike remarked, "Dang, that's bad."Mike then sat down and rewrote the rationale while Anthony continued to prepare posters for the performance. (Mike, Anthony's partner in this project, is a different student than the student named Mike who was introduced in Chapter 1.)

Framing and Reframing Problems and Questions

The modeling of the project process does not take place only in whole-class minilessons. Teachers and students need to work together continually to frame and reframe questions or problems for inquiry. A number of studies indicate that students, especially younger adolescents, need help in framing the questions for inquiry (see Marx, Blumenfeld, Krajcik, & Soloway, 1997; Moje, Brozo, & Haas, 1994). In addition, research shows that helping students frame and reframe questions is difficult work. It requires time and practice on the part of the teacher (Marx, et al., 1997).

The following conversation with two young men who were studying the problem of gang violence, graffiti, and tagging will illustrate how teachers can work with small groups of students to frame and reframe problems. (Tagging and graffiti are writing practices that tagging crews and gangs, among others, use. A tagging crew is a group of people who draw colorful characters on public structures. According to these students, tagging is different than graffiti because tagging is more like art. It consists of elaborately drawn, colorful characters and print. Graffiti, these students said, is often "thrown up" quickly and is used by gangs to claim territory). My experience supports Marx and colleagues' assertion that teaching students to frame and reframe problems is difficult work; I engaged in several conversations with Mike and Anthony, yet they still had trouble in their final presentation articulating the problem under inquiry. I noted that although they were working enthusiastically on their project each day, their work consisted primarily of writing about why they wanted to study gang graffiti and tagging and of drawing different tags and graffiti:

Elizabeth: Okay, my question is, Do you guys see tagging as a problem?

Anthony: No.

Mike: Yeah, for other people! 'Cause they have to pay to clean it up.

Elizabeth: Yeah. What I'm wondering is, if you don't really see it as a big problem, then isn't it going to be hard to write about it, Æcause you're supposed to write about it as a problem?

Anthony: No.

Elizabeth: Okay, here's something. Anthony, you don't see it as a problem, but Mike says it's bad for the people who have to clean it up.

Anthony: It is.

Elizabeth: So can you think of a solution? Like—

Mike: I don't think it's bad, but it's bad for the other people. I don't think it is, though.

Elizabeth: Right.

Anthony: Unless they tag on my house. (He smiles.)

Elizabeth: Oh?

Mike: Yeah, if they do it on my house—

Elizabeth: Then it's not good, huh?

Mike: Yeah.

> Elizabeth: So how are you going to resolve this little issue here? You're supposed to be writing about problems in our community, society, nation, and/or world. Okay, so how are you going to deal with the fact that you don't think it's really a problem, but you acknowledge it for the people whose places get tagged?

A first reading of this conversation excerpt might give the impression that Anthony and Mike did not have a strong sense of the problem that they were addressing through their inquiry. Indeed, they struggled to articulate a problem, and much of their classroom work seemed to involve writing and drawing examples of tags and graffiti for their performance posters. What I began to learn through this particular conversation, however, was that they struggled not because of confusion or sloppiness, but because of the complexity of the problem that they were trying to study and the complexity of the classroom context in which they were being asked to perform. In short, although they agreed with some of the social problems often identified with graffiti, Anthony and Mike wanted to distinguish gang graffiti from tagging. Thus, they identified two problems: (1) the problem of violence associated with graffiti; and (2) society's failure to understand the difference between the two forms and lack of appreciation of tagging as an art form. As they talked further, however, Anthony and Mike recognized that there were other problems associated even with tagging, as illustrated when they both suggested that tagging would not seem as artistic if someone tagged one of their homes.

In addition, the classroom context shaped what these two young men were willing to say. Although they had reason to trust me (we had talked about these issues on other occasions, and I had never revealed their knowledge to authorities), they were unwilling to express the full extent of their knowledge and commitment within the classroom and school walls. In other words, they said what they believed to be socially acceptable; they offered the socially acceptable version of the problem, even though they did not entirely agree with it.

Anthony, Mike, and I talked for a few minutes about things that we owned that had been tagged or graffitied. After a few minutes of trading stories, I pushed them toward discussing the problem:

Elizabeth: Okay, I'm going to leave you now. I want you to think about what you're going to do. How you're going to present this as a problem to be solved. Do you see what I'm saying?

Anthony: Eliminate it?

Elizabeth: Yeah, but what do you mean, Anthony? I mean, how can you get up there, you're gonna get up there and you're gonna say, "Tagging is wrong." Are you gonna say that?

Mike: What do you mean? It's not wrong.

Elizabeth: But what are you going to do? It's [the problem under study] supposed to be a problem in our society.

In this conversation I pushed the boys to define what they really thought of as the problem. As I talked with them I could see that they were thinking about tagging and graffiti in several different ways. I wanted them to think about how they would explain the problematic aspects of graffiti and tagging to the class, as well as offer suggestions for making change. We talked a bit more about their ideas for addressing the "problem" of graffiti and tagging, but their solutions seemed even more confusing. After more conversation, I discerned that although they did not really see tagging as a problem, Anthony and Mike did not understand that they could argue that people needed to be educated about tagging as an art form. They seemed to think that they had to offer ways to eradicate both graffiti and tagging, due probably to their sense they needed to give socially acceptable answers. I then encouraged them to think about ways to legitimize tagging in the public eye:

Mike: So all we're talking about is how we can resolve this problem?

Elizabeth: Right. Yeah, so how…I don't understand how you're going to solve a problem that you don't really think is a problem.

Mike: (after a brief pause) Gang violence is. It's a problem.

Anthony: Yeah.

Elizabeth: So you don't think tagging's bad, but you think that—

Mike: Gangs do tag!

Elizabeth: Right, but you don't think that—

Anthony:	Um, tagging, why don't they just tag on a piece of paper?
Elizabeth:	What? Why don't they just tag on a piece of paper? (Laughs.) Write that down. (He starts to write.) Or like what if, another idea might be to make a place that gangs could tag, or I mean that taggers could tag—
Mike:	There should be like programs for taggers—
Anthony:	They tagged in River Park, but they don't have it no more.
Elizabeth:	Like a big wall or something, you know, so you could tag on the wall anytime you wanted to tag.
Anthony:	Behind Soup and Stuff, they let you tag—
Elizabeth:	You know, like in bathrooms, sometimes they'll put chalkboards so that people don't write on the walls in the bathrooms…they like let 'em write on the chalkboards. What if they did something where, like, you could, you could tag a school, but it was done to decorate it and not to show violence?
Mike:	Yeah! Huh—
Anthony:	I can tag it—
Mike:	They should make characters, for like school, people walking to school, that'd be like bad, huh? School buses and stuff.
Elizabeth:	So write some of that down. Come up with some of those ideas. Like why don't they tag on paper. Why don't they create a place for people to tag? Why not use tagging in school?

We talked more about gangs and about their relationships with various gangs and tagging crews in the area. Then I pushed Anthony and Mike back toward framing the problem that they wanted to investigate:

Elizabeth:	Do you think that tagging crews are misunderstood?
Anthony:	Yeah.
Elizabeth:	Why?
Anthony:	It's just art.
Elizabeth:	It's just art. What about gangs, do you think they're misunderstood?
Anthony:	No.
Elizabeth:	Why not?

Anthony: I don't know.

Elizabeth: Okay, Mike, do you think tagging crews are misunder-
            stood? (Mike shakes his head "no.")

Elizabeth: Why?

Mike: What does misunderstood mean?

Elizabeth: Like do you think they have a bad reputation that they
            don't deserve?

Anthony: No, they don't.

Mike: Tag crews, all they do is just tag. But they don't have bat-
            tles, like cross each other. They don't fight each other. But
            sometimes they do, though.... But not as much as others
            do.

We can see a great deal happening in this conversation. We can see
that project-based pedagogy is responsive without being out of control.
That is, the pedagogy allows for student choice with teacher guidance.
Mike and Anthony chose to write about graffiti, tagging, and gang violence mainly because they liked to tag, mostly on paper and occasionally
on buildings. But they had chosen the topic to represent a social problem
and, in some ways they did believe that it was a problem. My conversation
with them helped direct Anthony and Mike toward articulating what they
saw as the problem under investigation, a problem that our conversation
indicated was quite complex and would need to be carefully articulated
(although they were not successful articulating the problem in their project performance, for multiple reasons [see Moje & Fassio, 1999]). To them
the main problem was the confusion between tagging and graffiti. Tagging was misunderstood as a violent act when to them it was an art form.
One problem to solve was that people needed to be better informed about
the artistic potential of tagging. In addition, taggers needed a space for
their practice. Gang graffiti, however, with which tagging was confused,
was to Anthony and Mike a violent and destructive act that needed to be
dealt with.

The preceding excerpt also illustrates some other potentials of project-based pedagogy. The opportunity to have a conversation like this allowed Anthony and Mike to collaborate with one another and to discuss
what is problematic in our society—and through this discussion to see

that problems might be defined differently by different people. With teacher support, they were encouraged to reason through the issue they studied and to obtain evidence to support their reasoning. Finally, they had a chance in their conversations and in their performances to practice communicative and rhetorical skills.

*Reflection Point*_____

Try to predict some of the problems or issues that your students might choose within the larger theme that you've chosen to frame your projects. (For example, in the air quality units that we're doing with middle school science students, the broad theme is framed by the question, "What is the quality of air in my community?" Within that theme, however, students might investigate the impact on the community of environmental legislation that would close or restrict certain industries.) With what would the youth in your classes struggle while trying to define problems? Develop a plan for a minilesson on how to frame problems within your theme.

Modeling Performances

Diane and I knew that these seventh graders had not had much experience with making formal presentations, even ones using only traditional forms of representation (such as reading a written report to an audience), and we wanted to encourage students to experiment with different forms like music, video, and posters. To provide a model for their performances, Diane and I each gave a performance well in advance of the students' performances. The following vignettes provide a glimpse of my performance for the class.

> Elizabeth stands in front of the room, while a popular song with the words "work that body" in it blares from a portable cassette player. Behind her on the chalkboard is written the title, "Work That Body: Deconstructing the Beauty Myth," and while the music plays Elizabeth dances

to the music, flexing her biceps and talking to kids in the front row. Students look at each other with somewhat puzzled expressions, and even a few smirks, while they watch her.

Then Elizabeth turns down the volume of the cassette player and looks at the class. "This morning, at 6:30," she says, "I was lifting weights. I dragged myself out of the bed to go to the gym. Why did I do that?"

Students shout out answers in response to her question.

"So you could be strong," said Jeffrey.

Mark said, "To get in shape."

"To look good," responded Katie.

Elizabeth picks up on Katie's comment. "To look good. Why? Why do I want to look good?" she asks.

As the class members offered possible explanations for my exercise regime—explanations ranging from "So you can feel good about yourself," to "So you can pick up men"—I listened and probed their responses, asking frequently, "Why? Why would that matter? Why do I think this is a good look to have?" By starting my performance this way, I modeled for the students a project performance that used music as a form of representation and as a discussion starter. My dancing around the room was a nice attention getter, but that was not my only goal. I wanted to emphasize for the class that I was giving a performance, something more than the reading of a report on research I had conducted. I also wanted to model for them ways to lead a discussion, so that the groups would try using audience participation as a central aspect of their performances. Next, I told the students explicitly about the kinds of materials, resources, and genres I used to prepare this performance.

> After about 2 minutes of discussion, Elizabeth uses a comment from Allan to move the discussion into the presentation segment of her performance. She says, "I'd like to focus on what Allan said, 'Because society tells you that's how you should look' to introduce my topic." She turns to the board, points to the title of her performance, and says, "These are all possible reasons for my focus on my body. But today I want to focus on the idea that we are told that it's important to look a particular way. I want to share with you my research about how the media—magazines, television, radio—tells us that we need to look a certain way and tells us what products to buy to achieve that look."
>
> Elizabeth picks up five posters that she's created from different magazine clippings. Interspersed throughout the visual images are quotes, in enlarged type, from the different books and articles that she's read.

> "Now, I have a report here, she waves a typewritten paper in front of them (see Appendix D), but I'm not going to read it because that would-n't get what I've learned across as well as these posters will. I've put information from the report on these posters, so that you can read some of the statistics that I've learned in my research."

Modeling the performance involved a combination of implicit and explicit messages. Diane and I have found that although modeling is critical to developing particular processes, practices, and tool use among students, modeling needs to be accompanied by meta-level explanations of what is happening in a particular activity. These meta-level explanations (such as,"Now I have a report here, but I'm not going to read it because…") help students understand why the modeler made certain decisions; it is not always immediately obvious to novices why and how people make certain decisions about the ways that they use language and literacy. Literacy educators often talk about using "think alouds" to model the cognitive processes involved in reading (cf. Haggard, 1988), but rarely do we discuss the importance of thinking aloud about the various literacy *practices* in which we engage. Diane and I tried to be as explicit as possible in our performances about both how and why we used certain tools and about why we made certain research or performance decisions, as illustrated in the next vignette.

> Elizabeth picks up her five posters and says,"I've prepared these so that they go in a certain order to show you how the media has gained more and more of a role in telling us how we need to look."
> Elizabeth then proceeds to talk through each poster, engaging the students in conversation about the different photos and what they mean in terms of the media's role in beauty and body image and how the magazines use bodies to sell products. For example, she shows the kids a clipping of an advertisement for jeans and says,"I'm going to stand way back here so you can't see the print. Okay, so this is an ad for?"
> Jeffrey answers,"Cigarettes."
> "Okay, we have one vote for cigarettes, or probably cigars..."
> "Yeah, cigars,"Jeffrey agrees.
> "Anybody else?"
> Amanda and Vance say,"Jeans."
> "How do you know?"
> "I read it," Vance says.
> "You, too, Amanda?"
> "No,"she replies.

"So have you seen this ad? Is there anything in it that made you think it was for jeans?"

Amanda says, "The shirt."

"The shirt? Why the shirt?"

"Whenever they have the shirt unbuttoned it's usually for jeans or something," she explains.

Jeffrey agrees. "The top of the shirt is always open."

"Oh, interesting," comments Elizabeth. "Amanda has already sort of incorporated a media image into her thinking; she knows that whenever they're trying to see jeans, the shirt—Tell me this, Katie, why is her shirt wet?"

"Ooooh, I don't know." Katie looks around at her friends and rolls her eyes.

"So it's see through," Mark answers.

"How does that sell jeans?"

"It makes her look sexy," says Jeffrey.

"Yeah...so they use like sex appeal to sell the product."

Jeffrey continues, "They're saying, 'This lady looks sexy so the jeans'll make you look sexy.'"

"If you'll buy 'em you'll look sexy," Mark adds.

These young people had a clear sense of how and why the media uses particular images to advertise or to shape the public's thinking and beliefs. As we continued to discuss the various images in each poster (which I had organized to show the historical development of the media's control over body and beauty image—a point that I made sure to share with students), I was impressed with the students' abilities to deconstruct the messages. When, for example, I showed a hair gel advertisement in which a young woman in a bikini chatted with two young men, one student countered my interpretation that the woman was wearing the hair gel so that she could attract the men's attention, with the interpretation that it could also send the message to men that if they would only wear that hair gel, beautiful, bikini-clad women would talk to them, too. The students were less clear, however, about how various news and information media consciously try to shape people's opinions of themselves as a way of selling not only beauty products, but beauty and fashion magazines and television programs. It was important that I made that point explicit, and also that I showed them *how* I made the point explicit as I prepared the posters and my written report:

Elizabeth also uses statistics to show that magazines have become more and more involved in creating particular images of beauty, mainly as a way to sell beauty products. She reads quotes from feminist researchers, news and research articles, and media historians, holding up the posters and pointing to certain images:

"Notice that they show bodies a lot. One historian says that as women started to move out into the work force and also in the 1970s and 1960s as people started adopting, like, different clothes as a way of rebelling, magazines started to focus more on body so that the number of dieting-related articles jumped from 60 articles in all of 1979 to 66 articles in *one month* in 1980. So all of a sudden a focus on body, on how you look, was more important than a focus on what clothes you wore."

Elizabeth notices that her performance is running long, so she hurries to wrap it up. She closes by sharing some of the findings of her own limited survey of students in the class and of her friends from the university. She reminds the students that she did the surveys and talks about how she tallied the responses so that she could report her findings.

As part of this portion of the performance I used visual images, statistics, and printed quotes to illustrate that the increase in eating disorders such as anorexia and bulimia correlates with the increase in media emphasis on beauty observed over the last 20 years. I illustrated how the magazines even seem to conspire in the focus on losing weight by placing articles on eating disorders next to advertisements of bathing suits. I used my own unsystematic data collection to add another layer to the performance, and to model the importance of considering personal experience and people in our everyday lives as sources of information. My interweaving of the images, the statistics, the quotes from research articles, and my own data modeled the ways that different aspects and forms of content information could be brought together in their projects and performances. As I introduced each representational form or source of information, I made quick comments about where I found them or why and how I used them.

Modeling the project—which Diane also did in much the same way—was extremely important to give the students a sense of what a complete performance could look like. We were lucky to have two teachers to model for the students, because our models of very different projects gave students more than one possibility for constructing their own performances. In both of our performances, however, we purposely talked about how we carried out certain tasks in the project, and about why we were doing things certain ways. So, for example, my point about not reading the report was as important as showing them that I had a written report. My comment about the visual images telling the story was critical to get students to think about the importance of other representations. I made a point to tell Mark that I had organized my posters in a certain way, so that he'd know they represented a type of photo essay and not just a collection of pictures. I read names of authors and titles of journals, books, and newspapers so that students would see that the information I reported came from multiple sources and from sources other than my own opinion or experience. I also showed students the surveys that I had done (letting them know that the surveys were informal and not systematic research), and I reported tallied results and interpretations, rather than just raw data. Finally, my performance consisted of me talking both *to* them and *with* them, so that students could envision these performances as more than just straight presentations.

Diane's performance, a slide show, which was significantly different than my presentation, also modeled the specific literacy strategies, practices, and processes that she used to complete both the project tasks and the performance itself. Because Diane conducted her project in collaboration with a student, she and the student, Stephen, were able to model a collaborative performance for the classes.

In addition to allowing us to model processes, practices, and tools of the project-based pedagogy, our performances had several other advantages. First, we were able to teach interesting and important content through our performances, and this would certainly be true in any content area. Throughout the discussion the students were attentive and even excited about contributing. They wanted to see the posters up close and they were eager to share their ideas. We even lapsed at times into hot debates about such topics as whether women should shave their legs and whether skateboarders' fashion choices are influenced by the media. (The skateboarders in the room claimed that they all "just dressed the way we want," whereas others—particularly young women—were "stupid" for letting the media tell them how to look.)

An interview with Anthony conducted later in the summer indicates that students learned important content from these projects. In the interview, Anthony explained that he liked the projects better than anything else in the writer's workshop class. When I asked why, he explained that he learned things that he had never known before from the project performances. Second, by going through something of the same process in which the students engaged, Diane and I were better able to predict students' struggles or to learn about them. We became members of a community of learners.

Reflection Point

What kind of project would you do if you were going to engage in projects with your students? How would you continuously model your process for the students? What steps would you add that Diane and I did not include?

Pros and Cons of Our Project-Based Pedagogy

Although we assessed the projects as useful tools for developing inquiry abilities in our students and for moving the students beyond a focus on individual writing, the projects were not perfect. Our list of advantages of using project-based pedagogy begins with the observation that most—but surely not all—of the students in the classes engaged in the projects with enthusiasm and motivation. Throughout the performances, we heard from male and female students who rarely participated in class, and we heard from students of all different ethnicities.

In a project performance on racism, students actually climbed out of their desk seats, which were arranged in formal rows, to turn and sit on the tops of their desk so that they could see each other—something they had previously groaned about when we had engaged in whole-class discussions. In general, students brought their experiences to bear on issues they had determined to be social problems. They combined a number of different forms of representation—writing, drawing, photography, video, music, and performance—to communicate their ideas, thus learning that meanings can be generated in many forms, while also transmediating their understandings of the topics of research and discussion across many different forms of representation. As a result of this collaborative work students were required to negotiate understandings and together construct new understandings, an important social and cognitive task. Students gained experience in locating, reading, analyzing, synthesizing, writing, and presenting information across multiple texts, including texts such as interviews, videos, drawings, and oral performances of other students and guest speakers. The students also learned to pull together a vast number of personal and published resources in order to make interesting presentations, while simultaneously learning how to design questions that would stimulate audience interaction. They learned these skills not only from our modeling through minilessons and performances, but also from participating in their peers' performances. These experiences provided critical opportunities for students to develop more varied literacy tools than they might have in a more traditionally conceived workshop approach.

Despite each of these positive outcomes, Diane and I noted a number of problems with the way we engaged students in project-based pedagogy. First, we found that our emphasis on multiple forms of representation led students away from developing well-written print texts, leading us to wonder whether students were able to develop conventional academic literacies that would help them negotiate future academic and professional contexts and cultures of power. As in the group project on graffiti and gang violence, many of the groups enthusiastically produced posters, videos, skits, and displays, but produced poorly edited written texts and failed to make connections among the different forms of representation. That is, their texts were compelling in terms of ideas, but were haphazardly written and somewhat unorganized according to standard writing conventions.

Second, we found that despite our requirement that students use many different information sources, student groups chose different forms of information to serve as the primary basis of their projects. Some groups consulted books and magazines and engaged in informal interviews with other youth, but never interviewed community leaders, parents, or teachers. Other groups only used interview data. Interestingly, no group used books as their sole source of information.

Finally, we were concerned with the discussions that took place during the performances. Not all groups were proficient performers, at least not according to mainstream conceptions of performance and presentation. Some voices were lost in the performances, and some performances consisted primarily of questions posed to the audience, despite the fact that each group had collected a substantial amount of information they could have discussed with the class. Some students' ideas were more highly valued than others, and a number of students were silenced.

On this score, our analysis of data indicates that the design of our projects—while driven by perspectives on collaboration, the co-construction of knowledge, and the importance of taking social action—did not really prepare students for or guide them in listening to others while also taking a voice, to be co-constructors of knowledge, and to develop relationships. In effect, we asked the students to examine large-scale community relationships, problems, and issues without first asking them to examine relationships they had with their peers in the classroom and school. We did not encourage students to analyze how their different social, cultural, ethnic, race, and gender experiences shaped the way they interacted with and related to one another. We did not teach them how to use literacy to further their relationships with one another or to examine social and critical issues. Nor did we prepare ourselves to be facilitators of such learning, hence the prevalence of what seemed to be authoritative discourses spoken by both adults and students in the room (see Moje, 1999). We put many structures into place to guide the enactment of projects, but we did not examine and address the relationships among people in the classroom.

Consequently, it seems that critical project-based pedagogy can only succeed if social-action projects are embedded in the idea that the work to be done in the classroom is work that will benefit and strengthen members of the classroom as well as people outside the classroom. To help students work as a group, it is necessary first to engage students in projects wherein they study who they are as a group of people, and how they live in relation to one another. The biographies with which we began the project might have been a first step toward such analysis of relationships. Unfortunately, we used the biographies only to teach interviewing skills, using them as individual narratives rather than as a tool for analysis of social positioning and relationships.

Students also need well-developed literacy tools to engage in project-based pedagogy. To revise our pedagogy with this in mind, we would engage in more explicit discussions with the students about the ways they research and represent the topics they choose. We would help them deconstruct and reconstruct various texts so that they could read and create a number of texts to examine the problems from different angles (see the discussion of how to use the K-W-L strategy in Chapter 7), and begin to situate problems in social relations, systems, and discursive practices. (For more on why this deconstruction and reconstruction of text is important, see Aronowitz & Giroux, 1991). Through these practices, students could learn to see the Discourses around them and analyze how different texts and Discourses can shape people's actions and future possibilities (see Aronowitz & Giroux, 1991; The New London Group, 1996).

During each of these activities, we would work with students to examine what they had identified as problems from various historical and political perspectives, questioning how the problems actually came to be problems. As classroom leaders we did not ask students to question the very problems themselves, and students found themselves confused about what the issues really were for them. In the gang violence and graffiti group, for example, we observed that the students talked about tagging and graffiti as misunderstood practices, but they also labeled these practices to represent economic and crime problems for society. Because they struggled to define graffiti and tagging in acceptable terms (i.e., writing on public spaces is bad), but found graffiti and tagging to be meaningful in their own lives, the group members and class participants had difficulty discussing steps that they would take to address "the problem." Similarly, a group who studied homelessness struggled between a perspective on homelessness as the fault of the homeless individual and a perspective that suggested societal responsibility in issues of homelessness. In future workshop revisions, then, we would model how to frame problems, analyze them, and look beyond explanations rooted in individual behavior or personality as a way of explaining problems, toward the material or discursive constructions of the issue.

Because of the difficult nature of supporting 8 to 10 different groups of students in one classroom as they engage in problem framing, reframing, and analysis, we would build multiple group performances into project work—performances that would occur throughout the project period. That is, students would engage in multiple dialogues, and we would use these dialogues as opportunities to reframe and analyze problems as a group. Students would be encouraged to examine many different ways that practices come to be constructed as problems over time and in particular social and institutional relations. Finally, Diane and I decided that in another iteration of this project-based pedagogy, we would build in performances throughout the term so that students would have opportunities to practice the performance genre and to learn from each other, while also building relationships with one another.

Project-based pedagogy represents only one way of being responsive and planful with our adolescent students in the classroom. It is a compelling pedagogical approach, however, because it begins with students' experiences, interests, knowledges, and needs. Project-based pedagogy provides guidance to students as they inquire about concepts and issues that they care about. At the same time, if the pedagogy is well structured—that is, if teachers are planful about introducing processes (such as K-W-L, concept mapping, interviewing, writer's workshop methods), practices (various ways of knowing, doing, reading, and writing), and tools (multiple forms of representation, different genres for writing), then students will be challenged to move beyond their understandings of the world, and they will learn the skills necessary for learning those new understandings. Using project-based pedagogy, or any other particular pedagogical strategy, does not guarantee that our students will learn, nor does it ensure that adolescents will learn literacy practices that can be powerful in the many different places they live and work. No pedagogical approach can accomplish this goal without major restructuring of school and society. Adopting some sort of pedagogical approach, however, rather than just using strategies and methods idiosyncratically, does provide a framework in which adolescent students can learn why literacy and content learning really matters. Perhaps by learning that what they do in and out of school matters, students will learn that *they* matter and that they *can* make a difference in the world.

Final Writer's Workshop Project Assessment Criteria

For this project, you will choose from two general themes: (a) important people in my life, or (b) problems or issues in community, society, nation, and/or world. (For example, Ms. Wilson is working on a project about her family; Elizabeth is working on a project about how television, movies, and magazines make people think they should look or act in certain ways.) You will work collaboratively in small groups, but you will be expected to make individual contributions to the small-group projects.

Each group will prepare a written paper and a performance. Group members will each contribute to both the written paper and oral presentation.

We will begin working on the projects on March 19. Class presentations will begin on May 16. Some of your work can be done in class and some will have to be done after school.

You will be evaluated over both the written and oral *processes* and *products*. Evaluation will be based on five qualities:

1. Content of the presentation:
   __ Is the content well organized and clear to others?
   __ Does the paper make sense?
   __ Does the presentation make sense?
   __ Is the information accurate?

2. Originality of the presentation:
   __ Is the paper interesting and written in a creative and unique way?
   __ Is the presentation interesting and presented in a creative and unique way?

3. Quality of the presentation:
   __ Is the paper put together neatly?
   __ Has the final draft been edited for spelling, punctuation, and grammar?
   __ Are the presenters prepared and serious?
   __ In the oral presentation, do the presenters speak clearly and slowly?
   __ Do the presenters encourage audience interaction and questions?
   __ Are the presenters prepared to handle questions from the audience?
4. Individuality:
   __ Can readers/listeners/observers tell that all individuals in the group made contributions?
   __ Did each member take responsibility for parts of the project?
5. Collaborativeness:
   __ Can readers/listeners/observers tell that the group members worked together to produce a cohesive and sensible presentation?
   __ Can the audience follow the presentation (oral or written), or does the presentation seem to be simply a collection of separate ideas?
   __ Can the audience tell that the group members consulted other resources as they worked on their projects?

Comments on Paper/Presentation:

Project Components

Components of Written Project (Check these off to make sure that you have included them.)

    __ Rationale
    __ Description of Process
    __ Body of Presentation
        __ Script to accompany a video, photo-essay, or dramatic production
        __ Narrative text
    __ Conclusion describing what group members learned and how they felt about the process
    __ Appendixes
        __ Process log—record of activities and research
        __ Interview transcripts
        __ Video
        __ Photos, slides
        __ Drawings
        __ Music CDs or tapes (list of them if the actual CD or tape is not available)
        __ References

Components of Oral Presentation

    __ Introduction or Conclusion (depending on how group decides to give the presentation) that tells:
        __ Why we did this project

    __ How we did this project
    __ What we learned from the project
    __ What the project made us feel about ourselves, our friends/family, our school, our community, our lives
__ Main presentation (could be any or many of the following possibilities):
    __ Video
    __ Dramatic presentation
    __ Photo-essay
    __ Performance
    __ Slide show
    __ Report reading

EVERY PRESENTATION MUST HAVE AN AUDIO OR VISUAL COMPONENT. For example, you could use drawing, drama, music, video, photos, dancing.

Elizabeth's Edited Project Rationale

I decided to do a project on how our images of ourselves, of our bodies, and of beauty are influenced by the media because I think that many of us are unaware of how much our thinking is shaped, if not controlled, by these media. People, both female and male, have many unexamined assumptions about what it means to be beautiful, and I think that these assumptions lead to negative and destructive behaviors, particularly on the part of women and girls. Naomi Wolf reports that "During the past five years, consumer spending doubled, pornography became the main media category...and 33,000 American women told researchers that they would rather lose 10 to 15 pounds than achieve any other goal" (Wolf, 1991, p. 10).

These self-destructive behaviors are not limited only to preoccupations with weight. Women are obtaining cosmetic surgeries—some of them quite dangerous—more often than ever before and the sale of cosmetic products has increased (Wolf, 1991). Wolf argues that cosmetics and an interest in beauty are not necessarily bad, but I believe that we need to confront our assumptions about beauty so that these assumptions do not destroy us.

I also have a personal interest in this project. I remember as a little girl being preoccupied with beauty pageants, Barbie dolls, and a model named Twiggy. Twiggy represented a major change in the way people thought about women's bodies and beauty. Before Twiggy, women were considered beautiful if they were shapely. With the advent of Twiggy (and other models like her), the image of beauty and bodies changed. No longer was a curvaceous body to be sought; instead, flat, thin, and bony bodies were admired as beautiful. The model Twiggy embodied this image, and I wanted to look just like her. I even had a Twiggy lunch box!

I have spent most of my life trying to look like Twiggy. My attempts to be flat, bony, and thin have been accompanied by some self-destructive and obsessive behaviors. I have also spent a lot of my energy worrying about how to straighten my curly hair (now that it is straight as a result of climate and age, I want it to be curly again) and how to darken my eyelashes, among other things.

I do not have anything against wearing make-up or attractive clothing, but I hope that this project will help me learn not to be obsessive about my appearance and will help others confront some of their obsessions and behaviors. In addition, I hope that this project will speak not only to women, but also to men, because men also worry about their appearances and because both women and men reproduce and support the beauty myth.

To achieve my objectives in completing this project, I am going to do the following:

- Collect photographs that show a variety of body images. These photos can be of famous people or of people I know personally.

- Collect photographs from magazines or photos of movie and television stars to show popular conceptions of beauty. For example, I could show a picture of Claudia Schiffer in contrast to a picture of Roseanne Barr to show how images of beauty are constructed in our society, because Schiffer is considered beautiful, whereas Barr is considered funny.

- Collect music about beauty and bodies. Nat and Corey suggested a song to me and so did Ms. W. I need help with other musical selections.

- Give a survey on conceptions of beauty and interview some of the people who respond to the survey. Use the results of the survey to help me write my narrative.

- Take slides of the photos that I'm collecting so that I can create a slide show. Use the narrative text that I write and the music that I collect to accompany the slide show.

- Read the books *The Beauty Myth* (Wolf, 1991), *Unbearable Weight* (Bordo, 1992), and *Volatile Bodies: Toward a Corporeal Feminism* (Grosz, 1994). I'm also looking for other readings on gender and beauty.

Appendix D

Work That Body: Deconstructing the Beauty Myth

by Elizabeth Moje

We are a consumer nation. We buy things to make us feel and look good. The media (magazines, newspapers, television, and movies) provide us with images of what we "should" be: wealthy, dressed in particular ways, beautiful, physically fit. Not only does the media push us to buy, but it also tells us what to buy. Our media system creates desires and fears among people—the desire to have certain clothes or the fear of being fat, for instance—and then capitalizes on those desires and fears in marketing and advertising campaigns. We are caught in a circle created by business and media. This circle is particularly vicious for women, who represent the largest magazine consumer market.

A recent *Wall Street Journal* article stated that the magazine *Cosmopolitan* alone has a readership of 15 million people worldwide, the majority of them women. Because women are such a strong force in the magazine industry, the advertisements and articles in magazines are designed to promote certain ways of thinking about women's bodies, beauty, clothing, and health (although they also show us particular images of men, as well). According to Naomi Wolf, author of *The Beauty Myth* (1991), after World War II, as women began to occupy not only domestic positions in the home, but also positions in the broader work force, businesses that had capitalized on domestic pursuits of women began to create a market that would maintain women's positions as consumers. That market was beauty and body. Magazines and other media were extremely willing to comply because they too needed to maintain the consumer-ship of women readers.

I decided to do a project on how our images of ourselves, of our bod-ies, and of beauty are influenced by the media because I think that many of us are unaware of how much our thinking is shaped, if not controlled, by these media. People, both female and male, have many unexamined assumptions about what it means to be beautiful, and I think that these assumptions lead to negative and destructive behaviors, particularly on the part of women and girls. Wolf reports that "During the past five years, consumer spending doubled, pornography became the main media cat-egory...and 33,000 American women told researchers that they would rather lose 10 to 15 pounds than achieve any other goal" (Wolf, 1991, p. 10). Lakoff and Scherr (1984) found that college women defined beauty in terms of health, energy, and self-confidence. However, when asked what an overriding concern was in their lives, the women responded that they wanted to lose between 5 and 25 pounds, even though none of them was overweight. "They went into great detail about every flaw in their anatomies, and told of the great disgust they felt every time they looked in the mirror."

And in a survey of 494 middle-class schoolgirls in San Francisco, more than half of the girls described themselves as overweight, while only 15 percent were so by medical standards. Eighty-one percent of the 10-year-olds surveyed described themselves as dieters (cited in Wolf, 1991, p. 215). Many of these young women are dieting at ridiculously young ages, ages when children need high levels of calcium, protein, carbohydrates, and some fats for proper physical development. Moreover, many of these young women are also engaging in starvation and binging-and-purging regimes that wrack their small bodies and stunt their physical and psy-chological development.

Peggy Orenstein, author of *Schoolgirls* (1994), tells the story of Evie, a 12-year-old girl who engaged in eating behaviors commonly associated with bulimia, a disorder in which people—usually females, because 90 to 95 percent of the people with eating disorders are female—eat great quantities of food and then "purge" what they have eaten by either vom-iting it back out of their stomachs or by engaging in intensive exercise regimes. Some borderline bulimics follow a less drastic, but no less detrimental, pattern: They eat excessively for one or two weeks (or days), and then literally eat nothing for an equivalent amount of time. (Read extended clip of Evie story here.)

These self-destructive behaviors are not limited only to preoccupations with weight. Women are obtaining cosmetic surgeries—some of them quite dangerous—more often than ever before and the sale of cosmetic products has increased (Wolf, 1991). One of the most dangerous cosmetic surgeries is breast enhancement. Breast enhancement usually involves the implant of silicone sacks that enlarge or lift women's breasts. Many breast implant surgeries have been conducted in the United States, despite recently revealed safety risks. A number of women have obtained breast implants, only to have the silicone sacks rupture, causing great risk to their health. Scientists have also raised questions about the possibility of an increased risk of breast cancer for women with surgical implants. Nevertheless, the majority of models and actors have undergone these, and other, potentially dangerous surgeries. When all our media images—models and actors—have perfect bodies, it becomes difficult for "ordinary" people to develop a sense of self that does not revolve around perfection. Stars who have face lifts as they age, for example, make us believe that we too should not age. Models with perfect hair make us wonder, "What's wrong with my hair? Why can't I ever make it look like that?" (Show photos of stars who have engaged in cosmetic surgeries).

As Wolf argues, cosmetics and an interest in beauty are not necessarily bad, but I believe that we need to confront our assumptions about beauty so that these assumptions do not destroy us. I remember several occasions in which I asked my hairdresser to cut my hair according to a picture I had seen and to help me learn how to make it look like the picture. He would look at me and ask, "And will you have the three people that she has to follow you around with hairbrushes, hair spray, and a curling iron for touch-ups?" When we see these images of people in the media, we tend to forget that their bodies have been surgically altered, their photos airbrushed, and their make-up and hair done for them!

I also have a personal interest in this project. I remember as a little girl being preoccupied with beauty pageants, Barbie dolls, and a model named Twiggy. Twiggy represented a major change in the way people thought about women's bodies and beauty. Before Twiggy, women were considered beautiful if they were shapely. With the advent of Twiggy (and other models like her), the image of beauty and bodies changed. No longer was a curvaceous body to be sought; instead, flat, thin, and bony bodies were admired as beautiful. The model Twiggy embodied this image, and I wanted to look just like her. I even had a Twiggy lunch box!

I have spent most of my life trying to look like Twiggy. My attempts to be flat, bony, and thin were accompanied by some self-destructive and obsessive behaviors. I have also spent a lot of my energy worrying about how to straighten my curly hair (now that it is straight as a result of climate and age, I want it to be curly again) and how to darken my eyelashes, among other things. I do not have anything against wearing make-up or attractive clothing, but I hope that this project will help me learn not to be obsessive about my appearance and will help others confront some of their obsessions and behaviors. In addition, I hope that this project will speak not only to women, but also to men, because men also worry about their appearances and because both women and men reproduce and support the beauty myth.

The good news that I can report from doing my project is that most of the people I surveyed included a number of characteristics or qualities that went beyond the physical as they described the beautiful people they thought of or knew personally. Although hair, eyes, skin, body, and clothes were mentioned several times in the surveys, people also mentioned qualities like kindness, humor, caring, generosity, sensitivity, wisdom, and voice. These results are encouraging, but it is important to note that only 2 people of the 50 surveyed chose to describe a man as beautiful. What would the characteristics of beauty be if we were describing men? Are there different characteristics for women than for men? For example, one of the respondents, a 37-year old woman, said this about her "beautiful" friend: "She is a classic beauty. She is tall, thin, and needs no make up. She is naturally beautiful. She has a very feminine, soft appearance, yet she is athletic and strong. She walks down the street and causes car crashes!" Although this sounds like a wonderful description, it is focused on the physical. It also sets women up as only being beautiful if they maintain a sense of "femininity." What if this woman were only athletic and strong? Would she then be beautiful? How would a man be described? Would his beauty have to be natural? Would it be more important for him to be strong and athletic?

I believe that these are important questions that we need to ask ourselves. We also need to ask about where these images are generated. Who shapes our thinking about beauty and body? Can we be happy with ourselves, even if we are not "natural beauties"? Most important, how can we maintain a sense of balance in trying to look and feel good, and have a healthy body and mind?

References

Allende, I. (1985). *The house of the spirits*. (1st American ed.). New York: Knopf.

Alvarez, J. (1992). *How the García girls lost their accents*. New York: Plume.

Alvermann, D.E. (1995/1996). Peer-led discussions: Whose interests are served? *Journal of Adolescent and Adult Literacy*, *39*(4), 282–289.

Alvermann, D.E., Dillon, D.R., & O'Brien, D.G. (1987). *Using discussion to promote reading comprehension*. Newark, DE: International Reading Association.

Ames, C. (1984). Competitive, cooperative, and individualistic goal structures: A cognitive-motivational analysis. In R.E. Ames & C. Ames (Eds.), *Research on motivation in education* (Vol. 1). San Diego: Academic Press.

Andrews, V.C. (1979). *Flowers in the attic*. New York: Simon & Schuster.

Anyon, J. (1981). Social class and school knowledge. *Curriculum Inquiry*, *11*(1), 3–42.

Aronowitz, S., & Giroux, H.A. (1991). *Postmodern education: Politics, culture, and social criticism*. Minneapolis, MN: University of Minnesota Press.

Astor, R.A., Meyer, H.A., Behre, W.J. (1999). Unowned places and times: Maps and interviews about violence in high schools. *American Educational Research Journal*, *36*(1), 3–42.

Atwell, N. (1987). *In the middle: Writing, reading & learning with adolescents*. Portsmouth, NH: Heinemann.

Baca, J.S., Iacone, J., Mutrux, F., & Thomas, R. (1993). *Bound by Honor (Blood In, Blood Out)* [Movie]. Los Angeles: J.S. Baca , T. Hackford, J. Iacone, S. Leopold.

Ball, S., & Lacey, C. (1984). Subject disciplines as the opportunity for a group action: A measured critique of subject sub-cultures. In A. Hargreaves & P. Woods (Eds.), *Classrooms and staffrooms: The sociology of teachers and teaching* (pp. 234–244). Milton Keynes, UK: Open University Press.

Barton, D. (1994). *Literacy: An introduction to the ecology of written language*. Oxford, UK: Blackwell Publishers.

Barton, J. (1995). Conducting effective classroom discussions. *Journal of Reading*, *38*(5), 346–350.

Bean, T.W., Bean, S., & Bean, K.F. (1999). Intergenerational conversations and two adolescents' multiple literacies: Implications for redefining content area literacy. *Journal of Adolescent & Adult Literacy*, *42*(6), 438–448.

Bizzell, P. (1982). *Academic discourse and critical consciousness*. Pittsburgh: University of Pittsburgh Press.

Bloome, D. (1989). *Classrooms and literacy.* Norwood, NJ: Ablex.

Bordo, S. (1993). *Unbearable weight: Feminism, Western culture, and the body.* Berkeley, CA: University of California Press.

Cameron, J. (1997). *Titanic* [Film]. Hollywood, CA: Lightstorm Entertainment Production (20th Century Fox and Paramount).

Cairney, T., & Ruge, J. (1998). *Community literacy practices and schooling: Towards effective support for students.* Canberra City, ACT: Commonwealth Department of Employment, Education, Training, and Youth Affairs.

Camitta, M. (1993). Vernacular writing: Varieties of literacy among Philadelphia high school students. In B.V. Street (Ed.), *Cross-cultural approaches to literacy* (pp. 228–246). Cambridge, UK: Cambridge University Press.

Cazden, C.B. (1988). *Classroom discourse: The language of teaching and learning.* Portsmouth, NH: Heinemann.

Collins, K. (1999). *Do you think I'm proper? A case study of educational exclusion and the social construction of ability, achievement, and identity.* Unpublished doctoral dissertation, University of Michigan, Ann Arbor, MI.

Connell, J.P., Spencer, M.B., & Aber, J.L. (1994). Educational risk and resilience in African American youth: Context, self, action, and outcomes in school. *Child Development, 65*(2), 493–506.

Connell, J.P., & Wellborn, J.G. (1991). Competence, autonomy, and relatedness: A motivational analysis of self-system processes. In M.R. Gunnar & L.A. Srouffe (Eds.), *The Minnesota symposia on child psychology.* Hillsdale, NJ: Erlbaum.

Cummins, J. (1984). *Bilingualism and special education: Issues in assessment and pedagogy.* Boston: College-Hill.

Davies, B. (1989). *Frogs and snails and feminist tales: Preschool children and gender.* Sydney, Australia; Boston, MA: Allen & Unwin.

Delpit, L.D. (1988). The silenced dialogue: Power and pedagogy in educating other people's children. *Harvard Educational Review, 58*(3), 280–298.

Dewey, J. (1916). *Democracy and education: An introduction to the philosophy of education.* New York: Macmillan.

Dillon, D.R. (1989). Showing them that I want them to learn and that I care about who they are: A microethnography of the social organization of a secondary low-track English-reading classroom. *American Educational Research Journal, 26,* 227–259.

Dillon, D.R., O'Brien, D.G., Moje, E.B., & Stewart, R.A. (1994). Literacy learning in secondary school science classrooms: A cross-case analysis of three qualitative studies. *Journal of Research in Science Teaching, 31,* 345–362.

Dillon, D.R., & Moje, E.B. (1998). Listening to the talk of adolescent girls: Lesson about literacy, school, and lives. In D.E. Alvermann, K.A. Hinchman, D.W. Moore, S.F. Phelps, & D.R. Waff (Eds.), *Reconceptualizing the literacies in adolescents' lives* (pp. 193–224). Mahwah, NJ: Erlbaum.

Dressman, M. (1993). Lionizing lone wolves: The cultural romantics of literacy workshops. *Curriculum Inquiry, 23,* 245–263.

Eccles, J.S., Adler, T.F., Futterman, R., Goff, S.B., Kaczala, C.M., Meece, J.L., & Midgley, C. (1983). Expectancies, values, and academic behaviors. In J.T. Spence (Ed.), *Achievement and achievement motives: Psychological and socio-logical approaches* (pp. 75–146). San Francisco: W.H. Freedman.

Eccles, J.S., Lord, S., & Midgley, C. (1991). What are we doing to early adolescents? The impact of educational contexts on early adolescents. *American Journal of Education, 99*(4), 521–542.

Eccles, J.S., & Midgley, C. (1989). Stage/environment fit: Developmentally ap-propriate classrooms for early adolescents. In R.E. Ames & C. Ames (Eds.), *Research on motivation in education* (Vol. 3, pp. 139–185). New York: Acade-mic Press.

Eccles, J.S., Midgley, C., Wigfield, A., Miller-Buchannan, C., Reuman, D., Flana-gan, C., & MacIver, D. (1993). Development during adolescence: The impact of stage-environment fit on young adolescents' experiences in schools and families. *American Psychologist, 48,* 90–101.

Eccles, J.S., Wigfield, A., Midgley, C., Reuman, D., MacIver, D., & Feldlaufer, H. (1993). Negative effects of traditional middle schools on students' motiva-tion. *The Elementary School Journal, 93,* 553–574.

Eckert, P. (1989). *Jocks and burnouts: Social categories and identity in the high school.* New York: Teachers College, Columbia University.

Eisner, E.W. (1994). *Cognition and curriculum reconsidered.* (2nd ed.). New York: Teachers College Press.

Erickson, F. (1986). Qualitative methods in research on teaching. In M.C. Wit-trock (Ed.), *Handbook of research on teaching* (Vol. 3, pp. 119–161). New York: Macmillan.

Evans, K.S. (1996). A closer look at literature discussion groups: The influence of gender on student response and discourse. *The New Advocate, 9,* 183–196.

Fairclough, N. (1992). *Discourse and social change.* Cambridge, MA: Polity Press.

Farrell, E.W. (1990). *Hanging in and dropping out: Voices of at-risk high school stu-dents.* New York: Teachers College Press.

Farrell, E.W. (1994). *Self and school success: Voices and lore of inner-city students.* Albany, NY: State University of New York Press.

Fassio, K.J. (1999). *The politics of young students' lives and literacy practices.* Un-published doctoral dissertation, University of Utah, Salt Lake City, UT.

Fenstermacher, G.D. (1992). The concepts of method and manner in teaching. In F. Oser, A. Dick, & J.L. Patry (Eds.), *Effective and responsible teaching: The new synthesis* (pp. 95–108). San Francisco: Jossey-Bass.

Fenstermacher, G.D., & Soltis, J.F. (1998). *Approaches to teaching* (3rd ed.). New York: Teachers College Press.

Finders, M.J. (1996). "Just girls": Literacy and allegiance in junior high school. *Written Communication, 13,* 93–129.

Finders, M.J. (1998/1999). Raging hormones: Stories of adolescence and impli-cations for teacher preparation. *Journal of Adolescent & Adult Literacy, 42*(4), 252–263.

Fordham, S. (1996). *Blacked out: Dilemmas of race, identity, and success at Capital High*. New York: Routledge.

Freire, P. (1970). *Pedagogy of the oppressed*. New York: Continuum.

Gee, J.P. (1996). *Social linguistics and literacies: Ideology in discourses* (2nd ed.). London: Falmer.

Gee, J.P., Michaels, S., & O'Connor, M.C. (1992). Discourse analysis. In M.D. LeCompte, W.L. Millroy, & J. Preissle (Eds.), *The handbook of qualitative research in education* (pp. 227–291). San Diego: Academic Press.

Glaser, B.G., & Strauss, A.L. (1967). *The discovery of grounded theory: Strategies for qualitative research.* New York: Aldine.

Goodlad, J.I. (1984). *A place called school: Prospects for the future*. New York: McGraw-Hill.

Grisham, J. (1995). *The rainmaker* (1st ed.). New York: Doubleday.

Grosz, E.A. (1994). *Volatile bodies: Toward a corporeal feminism*. Bloomington and Indianapolis: Indiana University Press.

Guerra, J.C. (1998). *Close to home: Oral and literate practices in a transnational Mexicano community*. New York: Teachers College Press.

Guthrie, J.T., & McCann, A.D. (1997). Characteristics of classrooms that promote motivations and strategies for learning. In J.T. Guthrie & A. Wigfield (Eds.), *Reading engagement: Motivating readers through integrated instruction* (pp. 128–140). Newark, DE: International Reading Association.

Guthrie, J.T., Van Meter, P., McCann, A., Wigfield, A., Bennett, L., Poundstone, C., Rice, M.E., Faibisch, F., Hunt, B., & Mitchell, A. (1996). Growth of literacy engagement: Changes in motivations and strategies during concept-oriented reading instruction. *Reading Research Quarterly, 31*(3), 305–325.

Haggard, M.R. (1988). Developing critical thinking with the directed reading-thinking activity. *The Reading Teacher, 41*(6), 526–533.

Haley, A. (1976). *Roots*. Garden City, NY: Doubleday.

Haley, A. (1992). *Roots* [Video]. Burbank, CA: Wolper Productions, Warner Home Video.

Hall, G.S. (1904). *Adolescence: Its psychology and its relations to physiology, anthropology, sociology, sex, crime, religion and education* (Vol. 1 & 2). Englewood Cliffs, NJ: Prentice-Hall.

Hall, S. (1995). The meaning of new times. In D. Morley & K.H. Chen (Eds.), *Stuart Hall: Critical dialogues in cultural studies* (pp. 223–337). New York: Routledge.

Heath, S.B. (1983). *Ways with words: Language, life, and work in communities and classrooms*. Cambridge, UK: Cambridge University Press.

Herber, H.L. (1978). *Teaching reading in content areas* (2nd ed.). Englewood Cliffs, NJ: Prentice-Hall.

Hinchman, K.A., & Zalewski, P. (1996). Reading for success in a tenth grade global studies class: A qualitative study. *Journal of Literacy Research, 28*(1), 91–106.

Hinton, S.E. (1971). *That was then, this is now* (1st ed.). New York: Viking Press.

Hirsch, E.D., Kett, J.F., & Trefil, J.S. (1987). *Cultural literacy: What every American needs to know.* Boston: Houghton Mifflin.

Hynds, S. (1997). *On the brink: Negotiating literature and life with adolescents.* New York and Newark, DE: Teachers College Press and International Reading Association.

Johnston, P. (1985). Understanding reading disability: A case study approach. *Harvard Educational Review, 55*(2), 153–77.

Kazemek, F. (1988). Women and adult literacy: Considering the other half of the house. *Lifelong Learning,11*(4), 23–24.

Kelly, M. (in press). The education of African American youth: Literacy practices and identity representation in church and school. In E.B. Moje & D.G. O'Brien (Eds.), *Constructions of literacy: Studies of teaching and learning in and out of secondary schools.* Mahwah, NJ: Erlbaum.

Kennedy, J.F. (1964). *A nation of immigrants.* New York: Harper and Row.

Knobel, M. (1999). *Everyday literacies: Students, discourse, and social practice.* New York: Lang.

Krajcik, J., Blumenfeld, P.C., Marx, R.W., Bass, K.M., Soloway, E., & Fredricks, J. (1998). Inquiry in project-based science classrooms: Initial attempts by middle school students. *The Journal of the Learning Sciences, 7*, 313–350.

Ladson-Billings, G. (1994). *The dreamkeepers: Successful teachers of African American children.* San Fransisco: Jossey-Bass.

Lakoff, R.T., & Scherr, R.L. (1984). *Face value, the politics of beauty.* London; Boston: Routledge & Kegan Paul.

Lankshear, C., Gee, J.P., Knobel, M., & Searle, C. (1997). *Changing literacies.* Buckingham, UK: Open University Press.

Lave, J., & Wenger, E. (1991). *Situated learning: Legitimate peripheral participation.* Cambridge, England: Cambridge University Press.

Lee, V.E., Bryk, A.S., & Smith, J.B. (1993). The organization of effective schools. In L. Darling-Hammond (Ed.), *Review of research in education* (Vol. 19, pp. 171–267). Washington, DC: American Educational Research Association.

Lensmire, T.J. (1994). *When children write: Critical revisions of the writing workshop.* New York: Teachers College Press.

Lowry, L. (1993). *The giver.* Boston: Houghton Mifflin.

Luke, A. (1993). Stories of social regulation: The micropolitics of classroom narrative. In B. Green (Ed.), *The insistence of the letter: Literacy studies and curriculum theorizing* (pp. 137–153). London: Falmer.

Luke, A. (1995/1996). Text and discourse in education: An introduction to critical discourse analysis. In M.W. Apple (Ed.), *Review of research in education* (Vol. 21, pp. 3–48). Washington, DC: American Educational Research Association.

Marx, R.W., Blumenfeld, P.C., Krajcik, J.S., & Soloway, E. (1997). Enacting project-based science. *The Elementary School Journal, 97*(4), 341–358.

McLaughlin, M.W., Irby, M.A., & Langman, J. (1994). *Urban sanctuaries: Neighborhood organizations in the lives and futures of inner-city youth.* San Francisco: Jossey-Bass.

McNeil, L.M. (1988). *Contradictions of control: School structure and school knowledge.* New York: Routledge.

Mercado, C.I. (1992). Researching research: A classroom-based student-teacher-researchers collaborative project. In A.N. Ambert & M.D. Alvarez (Eds.), *Puerto Rican children on the mainland: Interdisciplinary perspectives* (pp. 167–192). New York: Garland.

Mercer, N. (1992). Culture, context, and the construction of knowledge in the classroom. In P. Light & G. Butterworth (Eds.), *Context and cognition: Ways of learning and knowing* (pp. 28–46). Hillsdale, NJ: Erlbaum.

Merino, B.J., & Hammond, L. (1998). Family gardens and solar ovens: Making science education accessible to culturally and linguistically diverse students. *Multicultural Education, 5*(3), 34–37.

Moje, E.B. (1996). "I teach students, not subjects": Teacher-student relationships as contexts for secondary literacy. *Reading Research Quarterly, 31,* 172–195.

Moje, E.B. (in press). To be part of the story: The literacy practices of gangsta adolescents. *Teachers College Record.*

Moje, E.B., Brozo, W.G., & Haas, J. (1994). Portfolios in a high school classroom: Challenges to change. *Reading Research and Instruction, 33,* 275–292.

Moje, E.B., Willes, D.J., & Fassio, K. (in press). Constructing and negotiating literacy in the writer's workshop: Literacy teaching and learning in seventh grade. In E.B. Moje & D.G. O'Brien (Eds.), *Constructions of literacy: Studies of teaching and learning in and out of secondary schools.* Mahwah, NJ: Erlbaum.

Moje, E.B. (1999). From expression to dialogue: A study of social-action literacy projects in an urban school setting. *Urban Review, 31,* 305–330.

Moje, E.B., Collazo, T., Carrillo, R., & Marx, R.W. (2000). "Maestro, what is 'quality'?": *Language, literacy, and discourse in project-based science.* Manuscript submitted for publication.

Moje, E.B., & Fassio, K.J. (1997, December). *Revisioning the writer's workshop.* Paper presented at the National Reading Conference, Scottsdale, AZ.

Moje, E.B., & Shepardson, D.P. (1998a). Social interactions and children's changing understandings of electric circuits. In B. Guzzetti & C. Hynd (Eds.), *Theoretical perspectives on conceptual change* (pp. 17–26). Mahwah, NJ: Erlbaum.

Moje, E.B., & Shepardson, D.P. (1998b). Social interactions and children's changing understandings of electric circuits: Exploring unequal power relations in "peer"-learning groups. In B. Guzzetti & C. Hynd (Eds.), *Theoretical perspectives on conceptual change* (pp. 225–234). Mahwah, NJ: Erlbaum.

Moll, L.C. (1994). Literacy research in community and classrooms: A sociocultural approach. In R.B. Ruddell, M.R. Ruddell, & H. Singer (Eds.), *Theoretical models and processes of reading* (4th ed., pp. 179–207). Newark, DE: International Reading Association.

Moll, L.C., & Gonzalez, N. (1994). Lessons from research with language minority children. *Journal of Reading Behavior, 26,* 439–456.

Moll, L.C., Veléz-Ibañéz, C., & Greenberg, J. (1989). *Year one progress report: Community knowledge and classroom practice: Combining resources for literacy in-*

struction (IARP Subcontract L-10, Development Associates). Tucson, AZ: University of Arizona.

Moll, L.C., & Whitmore, K.F. (1993). Vygotsky in classroom practice: Moving from individual transmission to social transaction. In E.A. Forman, N. Minick, & C.A. Stone (Eds.), *Contexts for learning: Sociocultural dynamics in children's development* (pp. 19–42). New York: Oxford University Press.

Myers, J. (1992). The social contexts of school and personal literacy. *Reading Research Quarterly, 27,* 296–333.

New London Group. (1996). A pedagogy of multiliteracies: Designing social futures. *Harvard Educational Review, 66*(1), 60–92.

Nicholson, T. (1984). Experts and novices: A study of reading in the high school classroom. *Reading Research Quarterly, 19*(4), 436–451.

Nieto, S. (1994). Lessons from students on creating a chance to dream. *Harvard Educational Review, 64,* 392–426.

Noddings, N. (1984). *Caring, A feminine approach to ethics and moral education.* Berkeley, CA: University of California Press.

Noll, E. (1998). Experiencing literacy in and out of school: Case studies of two American Indian youths. *Journal of Literacy Research, 30*(2), 205–233.

Oates, S.F. (1998). *Literacy as everyday practice: A cross-case analysis of three sites of learning.* Unpublished doctoral dissertation, University of Utah, Salt Lake City, UT.

Oates, S.F. (in press). Literacy as an everyday practice. In E.B. Moje & D.G. O'Brien (Eds.), *Constructions of literacy: Studies of teaching and learning in and out of secondary schools.* Mahwah, NJ: Erlbaum.

O'Brien, D.G., Moje, E.B., & Stewart, R.A. (in press). Exploring the contexts of secondary and adolescent literacy: Literacy in people's everyday school lives. In E.B. Moje & D.G. O'Brien (Eds.), *Constructions of literacy: Studies of teaching and learning in and out of secondary schools.* Mahwah, NJ: Erlbaum.

O'Brien, D.G. (1998). Multiple literacies in a high school program for "at-risk" adolescents. In D.E. Alvermann, K.A. Hinchman, D.W. Moore, S.F. Phelps, & D.R. Waff (Eds.), *Reconceptualizing the literacies in adolescents' lives* (pp. 27–49). Mahwah, NJ: Erlbaum.

O'Brien, D.G., Stewart, R.A., & Moje, E.B. (1995). Why content literacy is difficult to infuse into the secondary school: Complexities of curriculum, pedagogy, and school culture. *Reading Research Quarterly, 30,* 442–463.

Ogle, D.M. (1986). K-W-L: A teaching model that develops active reading of expository text. *The Reading Teacher, 39,* 564–570.

Orenstein, P. (1994). *Schoolgirls: Young women, self-esteem, and the confidence gap.* (1st ed.). New York: Doubleday.

Pratt, M.L. (1991). Arts of the contact zone. *Profession, 91,* 33–40.

Richardson, V., & Fallona, C. (1999, April). *Classroom management as method and manner.* Paper presented at the American Educational Research Association, Montreal, Quebec, Canada.

Riis, J.A., & Leviatin, D. (1996). *How the other half lives: Studies among the tenements of New York.* Boston: Bedford Books.

Robinson, F.P. (1946). *Effective study*. New York: HarperCollins.

Rodriguez, L.J. (1993). *Always running: La vida loca, gang days in L.A.* (1st ed.). East Haven, CT: Curbstone Press.

Rogoff, B. (1990). *Apprenticeship in thinking: Cognitive development in social context*. New York: Oxford University Press.

Rosebery, A.S., & Warren, B. (Eds.). (1998). *Boats, balloons, and classroom video: Science teaching as inquiry*. Portsmouth, NH: Heinemann.

Ruddell, R.B., & Haggard, M.R. (1982). Influential teachers: Characteristics and classroom performance. In J.A. Niles & L.A. Harris (Eds.), *New inquiries in reading research and instruction* (31st Yearbook of the National Reading Conference, pp. 227–231). Rochester, NY: National Reading Conference.

Santa Barbara Discourse Group. (1994). Constructing literacy in classrooms: Literate action as social accomplishment. In R.B. Ruddell, M.R. Ruddell, & H. Singer (Eds.), *Theoretical models and processes of reading* (4th ed., pp. 124–154). Newark, DE: International Reading Association.

Scribner, S., & Cole, M. (1981). *The psychology of literacy*. Cambridge, MA: Harvard University Press.

Searle, C. (1998). *None but our words: Critical literacy in classroom and community*. Buckingham, UK: Open University Press.

Sender, R.M. (1988). *The cage*. New York: Bantam Books.

Shuman, A. (1986). *Storytelling rights: The uses of oral and written texts by urban adolescents*. Cambridge, UK: Cambridge University Press.

Siegel, M. (1995). More than words: The generative power of transmediation for learning. *Canadian Journal of Education, 20*, 455–475.

Silverstein, S. (1974). Where the sidewalk ends: The poems and drawings of Shel Silverstein. New York: Harper and Row.

Sizer, T.R. (1984). *Horace's compromise: The dilemma of the American high school*. Boston: Houghton Mifflin.

Stevenson, R.L. (1886). *Dr. Jekyll and Mr. Hyde, an inland voyage* (Copyright ed.). Leipzig: B. Tauchnitz.

Stodolsky, S.S., & Grossman, P. (1995). The impact of subject matter on curricular activity: An analysis of five academic subjects. *American Educational Research Journal, 32*(2), 227–249.

Street, B.V. (1984). *Literacy in theory and practice*. Cambridge, UK: Cambridge University Press.

Street, B.V. (1994). Literacy, culture, and history. In J. Maybin (Ed.), *Language and literacy in social practice* (pp. 139–150). Clevedon, UK: Multilingual Matters Ltd.

Street, B.V. (1995). *Social literacies: Critical approaches to literacy in development, ethnography, and education*. New York: Longman.

Tavake-Pasi, F. (1996, March 31). An important lesson for Polynesian parents. *Salt Lake Tribune*, p. A2.

Thompson, A. (1997). Surrogate family values: The refeminization of teaching. *Educational Theory, 47*, 315–339.

Thompson, A. (1998). Not the color purple: Black feminist lessons for educational caring. *Harvard Educational Review, 68,* 522–554.

Tilove, J. (1999, July 11). Closing the gap. *Ann Arbor News,* pp. B1–B2.

Venezky, R.L. (1995). Literacy. In T.L. Harris & R.E. Hodges (Eds.), *The literacy dictionary. The vocabulary of reading and writing* (p. 142). Newark, DE: International Reading Association.

Vygotsky, L.S. (1978). *Mind in society: The development of higher psychological processes.* M. Cole, V. John-Steiner, S. Scribner, & E. Souberman (Eds.). Cambridge, MA: Harvard University Press.

Walkerdine, V. (1990). *Schoolgirl fictions.* London: Verso.

Warren, B., Rosebery, A.S., & Conant, F.R. (1989). *Cheche Konnen: Science and literacy in language minority classrooms* (Report No. 7305). Cambridge, MA: Bolt, Beranek & Newman.

Wells, A.S., & Serna, I. (1996). The politics of culture: Understanding local political resistance to detracking in racially mixed schools. *Harvard Educational Review, 66,* 93–118.

Willis, A.I. (1995). Reading the world of school literacy: Contextualizing the experience of a young African American male. *Harvard Educational Review 65*(1), 30–49.

Wolf, N. (1991). *The beauty myth: How images of beauty are used against women* (1st ed.). New York: W. Morrow.

Wong-Fillmore, L. (1982). Language minority students and school participation: What kind of English is needed? *Journal of Education, 164*(2), 143–156.

Author Index

Subject Index